Exploring Filters with Photoshop CC 2017

Pradeep Mamgain
Soni Verghese

Exploring Filters with Photoshop CC 2017

© 2018 PADEXI Publishing. All rights reserved.

No part of this book may be reproduced, stored in a retrieval system, or transmitted in any form or by any means, without the prior written permission of the publisher, except in the case of brief quotations embedded in critical articles or reviews.

NOTICE TO THE READER

Examination Copies

Textbooks received as examination copies in any form such as paperback and eBook are for review only and may not be made available for the use of the student. These files may not be transferred to any other party. Resale of examination copies is prohibited.

Electronic Files

The electronic file/eBook in any form of this textbook is licensed to the original user only and may not be transferred to any other party.

Disclaimer

No patent liability is assumed with respect to the use of information contained herein. Although every precaution has been taken in the preparation of this book, neither the author, nor PADEXI, and its dealers and distributors will be held liable for any damages caused or alleged to be caused directly or indirectly by this book. All terms mentioned in this book that are known to be trademarks or service marks have been appropriately capitalized. PADEXI cannot attest to the accuracy of this information. Use of a term in this book should not be regarded as affecting the validity of any trademark or service mark.

Book Code: PDX001P

ISBN-13: 978-1986062350

ISBN-10: 198606235X

For information on all PADEXI publications, visit our website: www.padexi.academy

Contents

Acknowledgements v
About the Author vii
Introduction ix

Chapter F1: Using Filters F1-1
    Applying a Filter from the Filter Menu F1-3
    Working with Filter Gallery F1-3
    Applying Filters from the Filter Gallery F1-4

Chapter F2: Sharpening Images F2-1
    Tutorials F2-2
        Tutorial 1: Eliminating Camera Shake F2-2
        Tutorial 2: Sharpening Image using the Unsharp Mask Filter ... F2-5
        Tutorial 3: Enhancing Slightly Washed Out Image F2-7

Chapter F3: Working with Other Category Filters F3-1
    Tutorials F3-2
        Tutorial 1: Sharpening Image using the High Pass Filter F3-2
        Tutorial 2: Adjusting the Mask F3-4
        Tutorial 3: Creating Tileable Seamless Texture F3-6

Chapter F4: Creating Background Designs F4-1
Tutorials F4-2
Tutorial 1: Creating a Background Design - 1 .... F4-2
Tutorial 2: Creating a Background Design - 2... F4-3
Tutorial 3: Creating a Background Design - 3... F4-6
Tutorial 4: Creating a Background Design - 4... F4-7
Tutorial 5: Creating a Background Design - 5... F4-10
Tutorial 6: Creating a Background Design - 6... F4-13
Tutorial 7: Creating a Background Design - 7... F4-16
Tutorial 8: Creating a Background Design - 8... F4-17
Tutorial 9: Creating a Background Design - 9... F4-19
Tutorial 10: Creating a Background Design - 10... F4-21

Chapter F5: Creating Textures F5-1
Tutorials F5-2
Tutorial 1: Creating Marble Texture F5-2
Tutorial 2: Creating Door Mat Texture.. F5-5
Tutorial 3: Creating Military Camouflage Texture..................................... F5-10
Tutorial 4: Creating Leather Texture... F5-14
Tutorial 5: Creating Lattice Wire Mesh Texture F5-16
Tutorial 6: Creating Brushed Metal Texture... F5-18
Tutorial 7: Creating Reptile Skin Texture... F5-20
Tutorial 8 : Creating Sand Texture.. F5-22
Tutorial 9: Creating an Organic Texture.. F5-25
Tutorial 10: Creating custom diffuse, bump, reflection, and displacement maps... F5-28

Index I1

www.padexi.academy

Acknowledgement

I would like to express my gratitude to the many people who saw me through this book; to all those who provided support, offered comments, and assisted in the editing, proofreading, and design.

Thanks to:

Parents, family, and friends.

Teachers and mentors: Thank you for your wisdom and whip-cracking—they have helped me immensely.

I am grateful to many students at the organizations where I've taught. Many of them taught me things I did not know about computer graphics.

Everyone at Adobe [www.adobe.com].

Finally, thank you for picking up the book.

This page is intentionally left blank

About the Author

I'll keep this short, as I know your primary interest is how to create designs and textures using filters, not to hear all about me. I am a digital artist, writer, coder, teacher, consultant, and founder of PADEXI.ACADEMY. I am self-taught in computer graphics, Internet has been the best source of training for me [thanks to those amazing artists, who share the knowledge for free on YouTube]. I have worked with several companies dealing with animation and VFX in India. I love helping young aspiring 3D artists to become professional 3D artists. I helped my students to achieve rewarding careers in 3D animation and visual effects industry.

I have more than ten years of experience in computer and animation industry. I am passionate about computer graphics that helped me building skills in particles, fluids, cloth, RBD, pyrotechnics simulations, and post-production techniques. The core software applications that I use are: Maya, 3ds Max, CINEMA 4D, Photoshop, Nuke, and Fusion. In addition to the computer graphics, I have keen interest in web design/development, digital marketing, and search engine optimization. You can contact me by sending an e-mail to **pradeepmamgain@gmail.com**.

About the Contributing Author

Here is the contributor author in her own words.

Soni Verghese

I am a freelance digital artist, trainer, and instructor with years of experience in computer graphics and web design. I love working with computer graphics because the job never gets boring. There is always something new to learn or new ideas to implement. I thank the PADEXI team for their inspiration and professionalism. I thoroughly enjoy being part of the PADEXI team.

This page intentionally left blank

Introduction

Photoshop is not just about retouching images or manipulating photos; it can be used to create variety of textures, background designs, and effects. This book explains the tools and techniques available in Photoshop to create textures, background designs, and effects using filters. In addition, you will learn to create diffuse, reflectance, and specular maps for your 3D model. You will also learn to create seamless textures.

Each chapter provides step-by-step instructions for creating a design, there is plenty of room for explorations and experiment. You can follow book from start to finish, or do only the chapter that match you interests.

What are the key features of the book?

- Background design creating techniques explained.
- Texture creation techniques explained.
- Image enhancement techniques explained.
- Contains 25 plus standalone tutorials.
- Tech support direct from the author.
- Access to each tutorial's initial and final states along with the resources used in the tutorials.

Who this book is for?

This book is designed for the beginners and advanced beginners with an understanding of basic features of Photoshop.

Prerequisites

Before jumping into the lessons of this book, make sure you have working knowledge of your computer and its operating system. Also, make sure that your that you have installed the required software and hardware. You need to install Abobe CC 2017 on your system. Most of the tutorials will work in Photoshop CS6 as well. For system requirements and support, visit **helpx.adobe.com/photoshop.html**.

Exploring Filters with Photoshop CC 2017

Windows vs. Mac OS

This book is written using the **Windows** version of the Photoshop. In most cases, Photoshop perform identically on both Windows and Mac OS. Minor differences exist between the two versions such as difference in keyboard shortcuts, how dialog boxes/windows are displayed, and how buttons are named.

How This Book Is Structured?

This book is divided into following chapters:

Chapter F1: Using Filters, introduces you to the filters and **Filter Gallery**. You will learn how to apply filters from the **Filter** menu and **Filter Gallery**.

Chapter F2: Sharpening Images, shows the use of the **Shake Reduction** and **Unsharp Mask** filters to sharpen the images which is an image enhancement technique.

Chapter F3: Working With Other Category Filters, introduces the filters available under the **Others** category. You will learn to enhance an image using the **High Pass** filter, adjust the matte using the **Maximum** filter, and create seamless textures using the **Offset** filters.

Chapter F4: Creating Background Designs, introduces you to the filters and techniques used to create background designs for your artwork.

Chapter F5: Creating Textures, introduces you to the filters and techniques used to create textures for your 3D model texturing workflow.

Conventions

Icons Used in This Book

Icon	Description
💡	**Tip:** A tip tells you about an alternate method for a procedure. It also shows a shortcut, a workaround, or some other kind of helpful information.
📝	**Note:** This icon draws your attention to a specific point(s) that you may want to commit to the memory.

www.padexi.academy

Icon	Description
	**Caution:** Pay particular attention when you see the caution icon in the book. It tells you about possible side effects you might encounter when following a particular procedure.
	**What just happened?:** This icon draws your attention to working of instructions in a tutorial.
	What next?: This icon tells you about the procedure you will follow after completing a step(s).

Given below are some examples with these icons:

Note: High Pass Filter
*This filter produces the opposite effect that of the **Gaussian Blur** filter.*

Tip: Equalize Command
*You can also use the **Equalize** command from the **Image | Adjustments** menu. The **Equalize** command redistributes the brightness values so that they represent entire range of the brightness values.*

Caution: Clouds Filter
*When you apply the **Clouds** filter, the pixels on the active layer are replaced by the cloud pattern.*

What just happened?
*By specifying a value of **3** for the **Radius** option, we have expanded the white area of the mask to cover the blue haloing.*

*The **Roundness** option favors the roundness instead of secureness as we expand or shrink the mask using the **Radius** option.*

What next?
Now, we will boost the red and blue tones to pop those two color ranges in midtones.

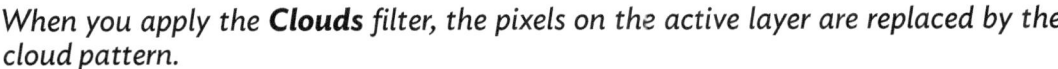

Important Words

Important words such as menu name, layer name, name of the dialogs/windows/panels, button names, and so forth are shown in bold. For example:

Ensure the **Base1** layer is selected in the **Layers** panel. Click the **Add layer mask** button to add a layer mask. Ensure the **Foreground Color** is set to **Black** and then pick a noise brush. Using the **Brush** tool, paint on the seams to get rid of them. When you paint black, you reveal the layer underneath.

Trademarks

Windows is the registered trademarks of **Microsoft Inc**. **Photoshop** is the registered trademarks of **Adobe**.

Access to Electronic Files

This book is sold via multiple sales channels. If you don't have access to the resources used in this book, you can place a request for the resources by visiting the following link: *http://www.padexi.academy/contact*. Fill the form under the **Book Resources [Electronic Files]** section and submit your request.

Customer Support

At **PADEXI.ACADEMY**, our technical team is always ready to take care of your technical queries. If you are facing any problem with the technical aspect of the book, navigate to *http://www.padexi.academy/support* and open your support ticket.

Errata

We have made every effort to ensure the accuracy of this book and its companion content. If you find any error, please report it to us so that we can improve the quality of the book. If you find any errata, please report them by visiting the following link: *http://www.padexi.academy/errata*.

This will help the other readers from frustration. Once your errata is verified, it will appear in the errata section of the book's online page.

IN THIS CHAPTER:

- Filters Overview
- Applying Filters
- **Filter Gallery**

Using Filters

Filters in Photoshop are used to clean up, retouch, and add special effects to the images. They can be accessed from the **Filter** menu [Fig. 1]. If you have installed third party plugins, these plugins will appear at the bottom of the **Filter** menu.

To use a filter, choose the desired filter from the **Filter** menu. However, you need to keep the following points in mind when you apply a filter:

- Filters are applied to the active, visible layer or to a selection.
- You cannot apply them to the **Bitmap** or **Index** colored images.
- Some of the filters only work on the **RGB** images.
- You can apply any filter to a 8-bit image.
- All filters can be applied individually. However, for **8-bit** per channel images, most filters can be applied cumulatively through **Filter Gallery**.
- Some filters are processed in RAM only. For such filters, you need to have enough RAM in your machine. An error message is displayed, if you do not have enough RAM.

Some of the filters only work on either 16-bit images or 32-bit images. The list of such filters is given next:

- **16-Bit Images:** Liquify, Vanishing Point, Average Blur, Blur, Blur More, Box Blur, Gaussian Blur, Lens Blur, Motion Blur, Radial Blur, Surface Blur, Shape Blur, Lens Correction, Add Noise, Despeckle, Dust & Scratches, Median, Reduce Noise, Fibers, Clouds, Difference Clouds, Lens Flare, Sharpen, Sharpen Edges, Sharpen More, Smart Sharpen, Unsharp Mask, Emboss, Find Edges, Solarize, De-Interlace, NTSC Colors, Custom, High Pass, Maximum, Minimum, and Offset.

- **32-bit Images:** Average Blur, Box Blur, Gaussian Blur, Motion Blur, Radial Blur, Shape Blur, Surface Blur, Add Noise, Clouds, Lens Flare, Smart Sharpen, Unsharp Mask, De-Interlace, NTSC Colors, Emboss, High Pass, Maximum, Minimum, and Offset.

Applying a Filter from the Filter Menu

You can apply a filter to the active, visible layer or to a smart object. To apply a filter, follow one of the methods given next:

- To apply filter to an entire layer, make sure the layer is selected and active.
- To apply filter to an area, make the selection.
- To apply the filer nondestructively, first convert layer to a smart object.

Now, choose a filter from the **Filter** menu. If a dialog box appears, change values and then click **OK** to apply the filter. If no dialog box appears, the filter is applied to the layer.

Note: Large Images
If you are working with a large image, previewing a filter effect can be time consuming. In such cases, to focus on an area, drag in the filter's preview window. Some of the filters allow you to center the image by clicking on the preview window. You can also use the + and - buttons in the preview window to zoom in or zoom out, respectively.

Working with Filter Gallery

You can use **Filter Gallery** to preview many of the special effects filters. Using **Filter Gallery**, you can apply multiple filters to the active, visible layer, smart objects, or to a selection. You can also turn on or off the effect of a filter, change the order of the filters, and reset a filter.

Caution: Filter Gallery
*Note that not all filters are available in **Filter Gallery**.*

Fig. 2 shows the **Filter Gallery** interface. You can open **Filter Gallery** by choosing **Filter Gallery** from the **Filter** menu. To zoom in or out in the preview window, click the **+** or **-** button or change the zoom percentage. These controls are available at the bottom-left corner of **Filter Gallery** [Fig. 2]. To pan in the preview window, drag in the preview window with the **Hand** tool.

> **Tip: Re-applying Filters**
> You can re-apply the last used filter by pressing **Alt+Ctrl+F**.

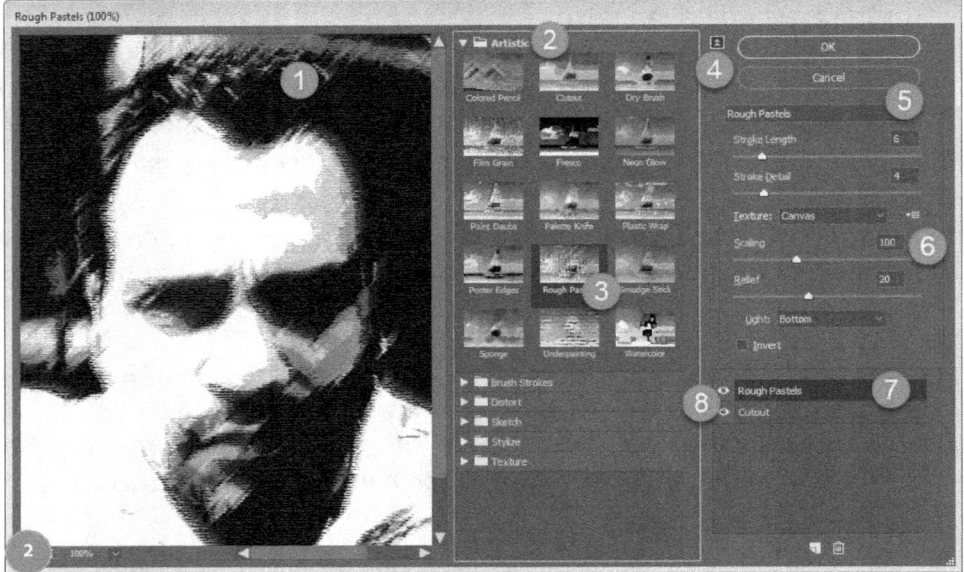

The table given next summarizes the interface elements of **Filter Gallery**.

Table 1: Filter Gallery Interface Elements	
Number	**Description**
1	Preview Window
2	Filter Category
3	Thumbnail of the selected filter
4	Show/Hide filter thumbnails
5	Filter popup menu
6	Options for selected filters
7	List of applied filters
8	Hide filter effect

Applying Filters from the Filter Gallery

To apply a filter from **Filter Gallery**, follow one of the methods given next:

- To apply filter to an entire layer, make sure the layer is selected and active.
- To apply filter to an area, make the selection.
- To apply the filer nondestructively, first convert layer to a smart object.

Now, expand the filter category, if not already expanded and then click on a filter thumbnail to apply the filter; the filter appears in the applied filter list in the lower-right corner of **Filter Gallery** [Fig. 2]. Now, change the options for the filter.

To apply filters cumulatively, click on the **New effect layer** button and then select additional filter to apply. Repeat the process to add more filters. To delete an applied filter, select it from the list and then click the **Delete layer** button. To rearrange the filters, drag the filter layer to a new location in the applied filters list. When you are done with the filters, click **OK** to apply effect to the layer.

Summary
In this chapter:

- Filters Overview
- Applying Filters
- **Filter Gallery**

This page is intentionally left blank

IN THIS CHAPTER:

- 3 Tutorials covering image sharpening techniques
- Covers the following filters: **Shake Reduction** and **Unsharp Mask**

Chapter F2

Sharpening Images

Sharpening is an image enhancement technique in which the contrast between the specific pixels is enhanced. In this chapter, we will explore some sharpening filters available in Photoshop.

Photoshop CC 2017

Tutorials

Before you start the tutorials, create a folder with the name **chapter-f2**. We will use this folder to host all the tutorial files and other resources.

Tutorial 1: Eliminating Camera Shake

In this tutorial, we will use the **Shake Reduction** filter to eliminate the camera shake [Fig. T1]

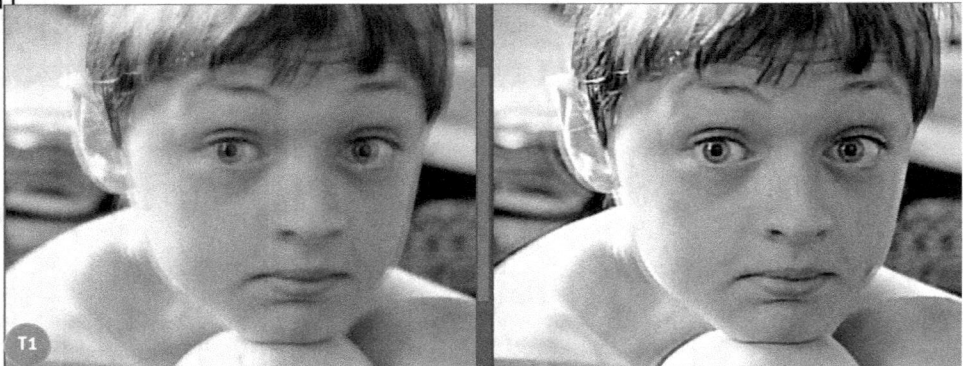

The following table summarizes the tutorial:

Table T1	
Flow: *The following sequence will be used in this tutorial:*	
1. Open image. 2. Apply the *Shake Reduction* filter. 3. Adjust filter options to get the desired result.	
Keyword: *Shake Reduction*	
Difficulty level	Beginner
Estimated time to complete	20 Minutes
Topics	• Getting Started • Removing the Camera Shake
Resources folder	**chapter-f2**
Final tutorial file	**f2_tut1_finish.psd**
Footage courtesy	**http://www.cairodar.com**

Getting Started

The **Shake Reduction** filter allows you to reduce blurriness in the image caused by the camera motion. This filter lets you reduce blurring caused by the several types of camera motion such as linear motion, arc-shaped motion, rotational motion, zig-zag motion and so forth.

Note: Suitable images for this filter
This filter works best with the directly lit still camera images having a low noise. It also sharpens the blurred text in the images. The following types of images are well suited for this filter:

- *Images captured using a lens with a long focal length.*
- *Indoor images taken with a slow shutter speed or without flash.*

Press **Ctrl+O** and then open the **asset-01.jpg**.

Removing the Camera Shake
Follow the steps given next:

1. Choose **Sharpen | Shake Reduction** from the **Filter** menu to open the **Shake Reduction** dialog box [Fig. T2].

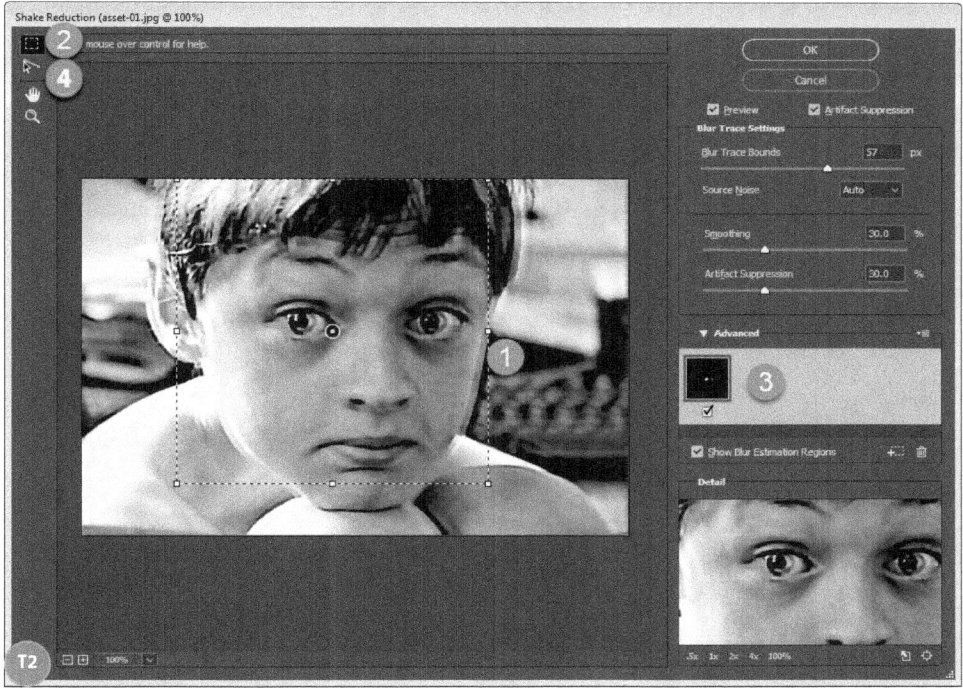

 What just happened?
*Photoshop automatically analyzes the region best suited for the shake reduction. It also analyzes the nature of the blur and then applies appropriate correction to the entire image. A rectangular marquee region is automatically created [labelled as 1 in Fig. T2]. You can resize this region by dragging any of its corners. The pin in the center of the area allows you to move the region to a different location. To define another region, you can choose **Blur***

Estimation Tool [or press **E**, labelled as 2 in Fig. T2] from the top left corner of the dialog box. To draw a new region, activate the tool and draw on an area of the image.

In the **Advance** panel [labelled as 3 in Fig. T2], a blur trace swatch represents the shape and extent of the blur that affects the selected region of the image. If you want Photoshop to further fine-tune the image, you can add multiple blur traces. You can also use **Blur Direction Tool** [Hotkey: R] available on the top-left corner of the dialog box to create a blur trace manually.

> *Caution: Preview*
> If no correction seems to be applied to the image in the dialog box, make sure to enable the **Preview** check box.

> *Tip: Detail loupe*
> The **Detail** loupe on the lower-right corner of the dialog shows the region in focus. Click on it and then release the mouse button to switch between the original and corrected versions. The **Q** key allows you to dock or undock the **Detail** loupe.

2. Place the blur estimation region, as shown in Fig. T3.

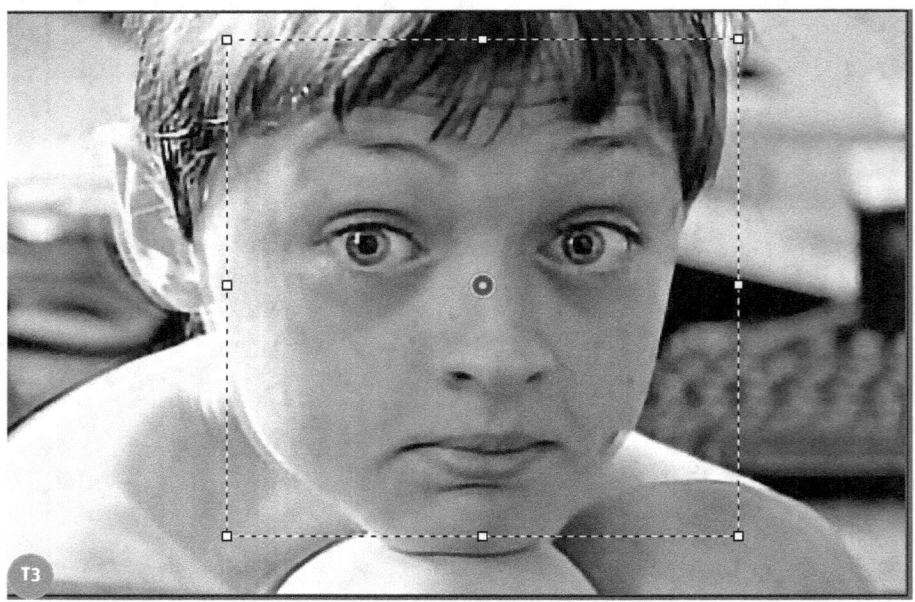

3. On the **Blur Trace Settings** area, change **Smoothing** and **Artifact Suppression** to **25** and **42**, respectively.

What just happened?
*Here, by changing the **Smoothing** value, we have reduced high-frequency sharpening noise form the image. The **Artifact Suppression** option suppresses the noise artifacts that can appear when we sharpen the image. It works best with the medium-frequency noise.*

4. Using the **Hand** tool, focus on the area of the image, as shown in Fig. T4. Now, click on the **Enhance at loupe location** icon.

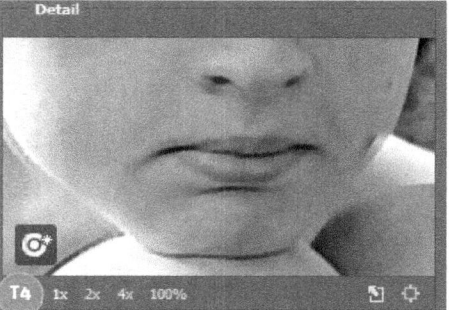

What just happened?
*Click the **Enhance at loupe location** icon to move the blur estimation region to the region highlighted in the **Details** loupe. By doing so, the blur trace for the region displayed earlier in the **Detail** loupe is automatically updated.*

5. Click **OK** to apply the filter. Save the work.

Tutorial 2: Sharpening Image using the Unsharp Mask Filter

In this tutorial, we will use the **Unsharp Mask** filter to sharpen the image [Fig. T1].

The following table summarizes the tutorial:

Table T2	
Flow: *The following sequence will be used in this tutorial:* *1. Open image. 2. Apply the **Unsharp Mask** filter. 3. Adjust filter options to get the desired result.*	
Keyword: Unsharp Mask	
Difficulty level	Beginner

Table T2	
Estimated time to complete	20 Minutes
Topics	• Getting Started • Sharpening the Image
Resources folder	chapter-f2
Final tutorial file	f2_tut2_finish.psd
Footage courtesy	Andrew Clarke https://www.freeimages.com/photographer/annastasia-40497

Getting Started

The **Unsharp Mask** filter allows you to sharpen an image by increasing contrast along the edges in an image. Note that this filter does not detect edges in the image. Instead, it detects pixels that differ in value from the surrounding pixels. You can control this value using the **Threshold** option.

Then, it increases the contrast of the surrounding pixels you specify. In addition, you can specify the radius of the region in which each pixel is compared. Larger the radius you specify, larger will be the effects on edges.

Caution: Larger radius value
If you specify a larger radius value, there will a halo effect around the edges. You can apply this filter to only one layer at a time even if layers are grouped or linked.

Press **Ctrl+O** and then open the **asset-02.jpg**.

Sharpening the Image
Follow the steps given next:

1. Choose **Sharpen | Unsharp Mask** from the **Filter** menu to open the **Unsharp Mask** dialog box [Fig. T2].

2. Change **Radius** to **6**.

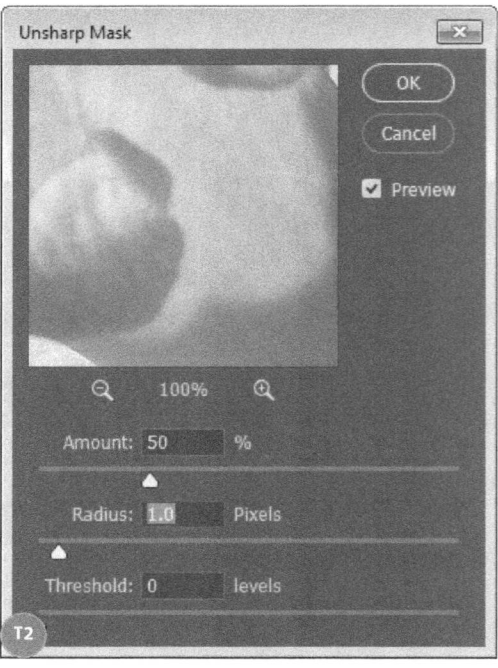

What just happened?
Here, I've specified the radius to determine the number of pixels surrounding the edge pixels that affect the sharpening. This value varies as per the subject in the image, size of the final image you will save, and the output method used. For high resolution images a value of 1 or 2 is generally recommended. A lower value only sharpen the edge pixels whereas the high value sharpens a broad range of pixels.

3. Change **Amount** to **100**.

 What just happened?
Here, I've specified a value that will determine how much to increase the contrast of the pixels. For high resolution images, a value between 150% and 200% is generally recommended.

4. Change **Threshold** to **6**.

 What just happened?
Here, I've specified a value that will determine how different the sharpened pixels must be from the surrounding area before they are considered edge pixels and sharpened by the filter. For example, a value of 3 affects all pixels that have tonal values that differ by a value of 3 or more [on a 0-255 scale]. The default value 0 sharpens all pixels.

5. Click **OK** to apply the filter and then save the work.

Tutorial 3: Enhancing Slightly Washed Out Image

In this tutorial, we will learn to adjust the color, contrast, and sharpness of an image to add some punch to it. This technique is useful in cases where image is slightly washed out. It is also useful in correcting objects that were close to the camera flash. Fig. T1 shows the original and corrected images, respectively.

The following table summarizes the tutorial:

Table T3	
Flow: The following sequence will be used in this tutorial: *1. Open image, 2. Use the color commands and **Unsharp Mask** filter to enhance the image.*	
Keywords: Shadows/Highlights, Color Balance, Brightness/Contrast, and Unsharp Mask	
Difficulty level	Intermediate
Estimated time to complete	30 Minutes
Topics	• Getting Started • Enhancing the Image
Resources folder	chapter-f2
Final tutorial file	f2_tut3_finish.psd
Footage courtesy	Style 74 https://www.freeimages.com/photo/zion-national-park-1331762

Getting Started

Press **Ctrl+O** and then open the **asset-03.jpg**.

Enhancing the Image

1. Press **Ctrl+J** to duplicate the **Background** layer. Photoshop creates a new layer with the name **Layer 1**. Now, change the blending mode of **Layer 1** to **Multiply** [Fig. T2].

Chapter F2 - Sharpening Images

→ *What next?*
Notice the image is dark. Now, we have to reduce the darkness, we will do so by using the Shadows/Highlights command and by adjusting the opacity of Layer 1.

2. Choose **Adjustments | Shadows/Highlights** from the **Image** menu. Set the **Amount** slider to **90** in the **Shadows** section of the **Shadows/Highlights** dialog box and then click **OK** [Fig. T3]. Reduce the Layer 1's **Opacity** to **48%**; Fig. T4 shows the result.

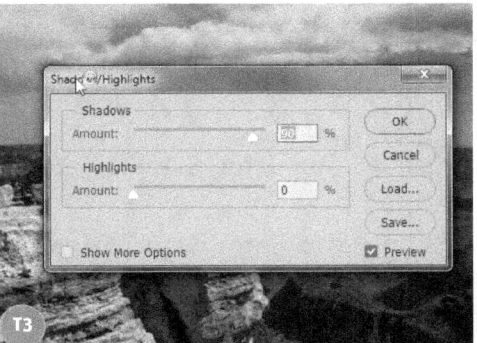 

In which situations the Shadows/Highlights command can be used?
You can use this command if:

1. *The image is washed out.*
2. *The objects in the images were too close to the camera.*
3. *You want to brighten the regions that are in shadows in a well-lit image.*

*This command is a pretty intelligent command. It lightens or darkens the pixels based on the surrounding pixels in the local neighborhood. The **Amount** slider controls the strength of the adjustment or correction. **Tone** gives you ability to control the range of tones to be adjusted. **Radius** controls the size of local neighborhood around each pixel.*

3. Press **Ctrl+E** to merge the two layers.

Tip: Non-destructive merger of the layers
You can use the shortcut key combination Ctrl+Shift+Alt+E to create a new layer which would be the merged result of the two layer we have. This way, you can work non-destructively.

→ *What next?*
Now, we will boost the red and blue tones to pop those two color ranges in midtones.

4. Choose **Adjustments | Color Balance** from the **Image** menu or press **Ctrl+B**. In the **Color Balance** dialog that appears, set the **Color Levels** to **0, 0, +31** and then click **OK** [Fig. T5].

   What just happened?
   The **Color Balance** command allows you to perform a generalized color correction. You can use this command to change the overall mixture of colors in the image.

   Tip: Composite channel
   Ensure the composite channel is selected in the **Channel** panel. This command only available when the composite channel is selected.

5. Press **Ctrl+B** again and set **Color Levels** to **0, 0, -15** and then click **OK**.

   Tip: Brightness/Contrast command
   If you want to give little more kick to the image, adjust the brightness using the **Brightness/Contrast** command.

6. Choose **Adjustments | Brightness/Contrast** from the **Image** menu. Anchor the **Brightness** slider at **18** [Fig. T6] and then click **OK**.

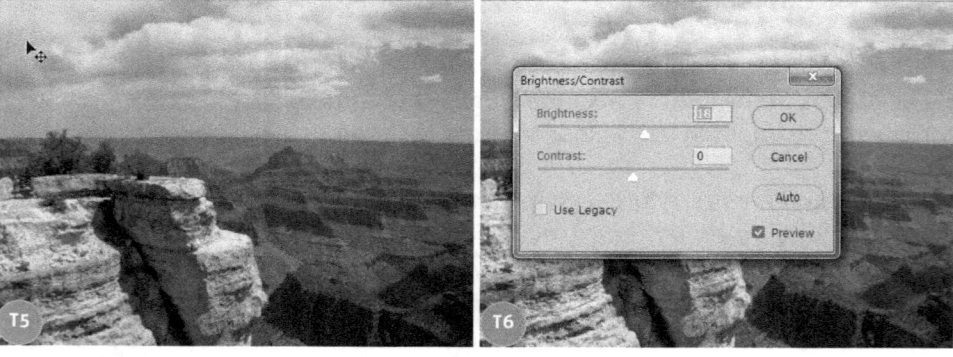

   Tip: Brightness/Contrast adjustment layer
   You can also use the **Brightness/Contrast** adjustment layer. If you use the adjustment layer you can mask away the areas which appear over exposed.

   What Brightness/Contrast command does?
   The **Brightness/Contrast** command allows you to make simple tonal adjustments. As you drag the **Brightness** slider to the right, it increases the tonal values and expands highlights. Dragging it to the left expands shadows. The **Contrast** slider allows you to expand or shrink the overall range of the tonal values.

What next?
Now, let's apply an **Unsharp Mask** to sharpen the image.

7. Choose **Sharpen | Unsharp Mask** from the **Filter** menu. In the **Unsharp Mask** dialog that appears, set the sliders as shown in Fig. T7 and then click **OK**.

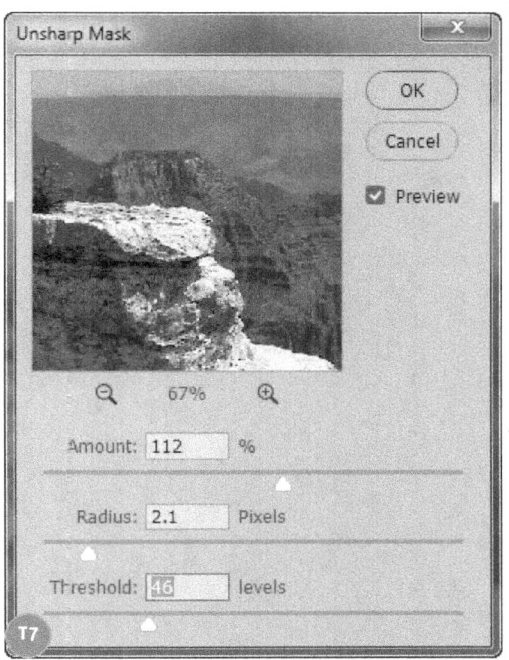

 What Unsharp Mask filter does?
This filter allows you to sharpen an image by increasing contrast along the edges. You should also understand that how this filter works. This filter does not detect edges. It locates the pixels that differ in values from the surrounding pixels considering the values you specify using the **Threshold** slider. It increases the contrast of the surrounding pixels by the amount you specify using the **Amount** slider. The comparison region is controlled by the **Radius** slider. This slider is used to determine whether a pixel is in shadows or highlights.

 Tip: Smart Sharpen filter
You can also use the **Smart Sharpen** filter which has some additional control.

Summary
In this chapter:

- 3 Tutorials covering image sharpening techniques
- Covers the following filters: **Shake Reduction** and **Unsharp Mask**

This page is intentionally left blank

IN THIS CHAPTER:

- 3 Tutorials covering filters from the Others category.
- Covers the following filters: **High Pass**, **Maximum**, and **Offset**

Working with Other Category Filters

The filters under the Other category are used to create your own custom filters, modify masks, make quick color adjustments, and offset a selection.

Photoshop CC 2017

Tutorials

Before you start the tutorials, create a folder with the name **chapter-f3**. We'll use this folder to host all the tutorial files and other resources.

Tutorial 1: Sharpening Image using the High Pass Filter

In this tutorial, we will use the **High Pass** filter to enhance the appearance of the image [Fig. T1].

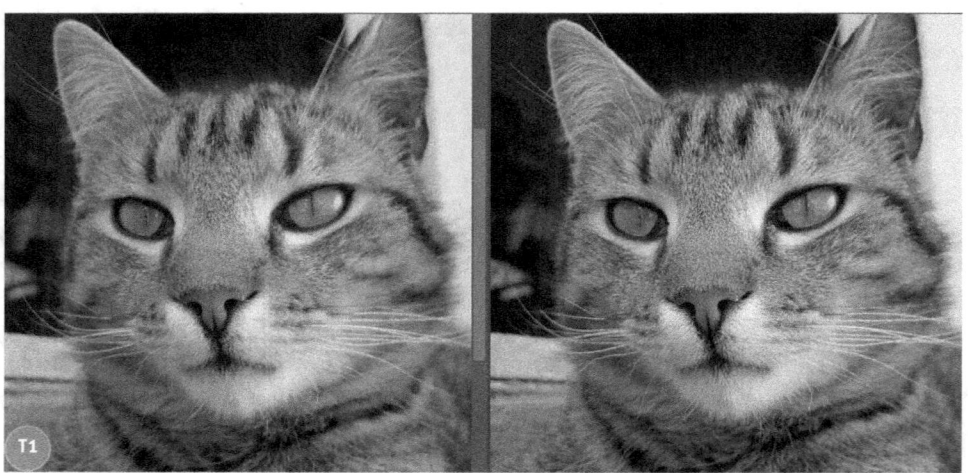

The following table summarizes the tutorial:

Table T1	
Flow: *The following sequence will be used in this tutorial:* 1. Open image. 2. Convert image to a smart object. 3. Apply the **High Pass** filter. 3. Adjust filter options to get the desired result.	
Keyword: *High Pass*	
Difficulty level	Beginner
Estimated time to complete	10 Minutes
Topics	• Getting Started • Sharpening the Image
Resources folder	chapter-f3
Final tutorial file	f3-tut1-finish.psd

Table T1	
Footage courtesy	Gabor Szakacs https://www.freeimages.com/photographer/sakman-36676

Getting Started

The **High Pass** filter allows you to retain the edge details where the sharp transitions occur and suppresses the rest of the image. This filter creates an effect opposite to that of the **Gaussian Blur** filer. It is useful in extracting the line art and large black and white areas from an image.

Press **Ctrl+O** and then open the **asset-01.jpg**.

Sharpening the Image
Follow the steps given next:

1. On the **Layers** panel, right-click on the layer and then choose **Convert to Smart Object** from the popup menu to create a smart object from the layer.

   What just happened?
   Here, I've converted layer to a smart object. Smart objects are layers that contain image data from raster or vector images. Smart object preserves the source data. Therefore, you can perform nondestructive editing to the layer.

2. Choose **Other | High Pass** from the **Filter** menu to open the **High Pass** dialog box [Fig. T2].

3. Change **Radius** to **2** and then click **OK**. On the **Layers** panel, double-click on the **Edit filter blending icon** [labelled 1 in Fig. T3] to open the **Blending Options (High Pass)** dialog box [Fig. T4].

4. Change **Mode** to **Overlay** and **Opacity** to **77%**. Click **OK** to apply the filter [Fig. T5].

   Note: Adjusting the Radius
   *Since, we've converted the original layer to a smart object, we can now change the **Radius** value. To do so, double-click on the filter name in the **Layers** panel [labelled 2 in Fig. T3]. Now, you can change the **Radius** value from the **High Pass** dialog box.*

Tutorial 2: Adjusting the Mask

In this tutorial, we will use the **High Pass** filter to enhance the appearance of the image [Fig. T1].

The following table summarizes the tutorial:

Table T2
Flow: The following sequence will be used in this tutorial:
*1. Open the start file 2. Select mask. 3. Apply the **Maximum** filter. 4. Adjust filter options to adjust the mask.*

Table T2	
Keywords: Maximum and Minimum	
Difficulty level	Beginner
Estimated time to complete	10 Minutes
Topics	• Getting Started • Adjusting the Mask
Resources folder	**chapter-f3**
Start tutorial file	**f3-tut2-start.psd**
Final tutorial file	**f3-tut2-finish.psd**
Footage courtesy	**Dragan Sasic** https://www.freeimages.com/photographer/sasicd-31575

Getting Started

The **Maximum** and **Minimum** filters are useful for modifying the masks. The **Maximum** filter spreads the white areas and erodes the black areas. The **Minimum** filter shrinks the white areas and spreads out the black areas.

Press **Ctrl+O** and then open the **f3-tut2-strat.psd**. This file has two layers. **Layer 0** contains a t-shirt in blue color. A **Hue and Saturation** adjustment layer is changing color of the t-shirt to brown using a mask. **Alt+click** on the mask swatch to see the mask in the work area [Fig. T2]. **Alt+click** again to see the color image.

If you zoom in on image, you will notice that there is a blue haloing on the edges of the t-shirt [Fig. T3]. Let's fix it using the **Maximum** filter.

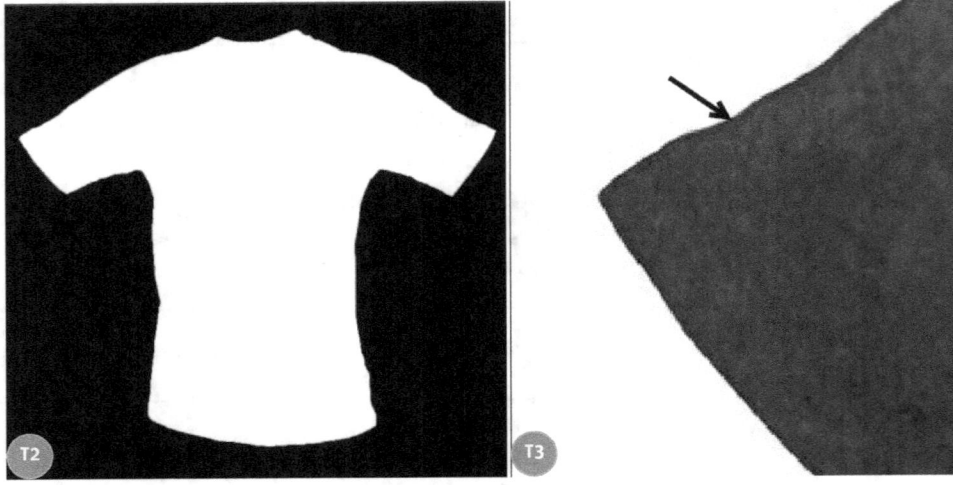

Adjusting the Mask

Follow the steps given next:

1. On the **Layers** panel, make sure that the mask swatch is selected and then choose **Other | Maximum** from the **Filter** menu to open the **Maximum** dialog box.

2. On this dialog box, change **Radius** to **3** and **Preserve** to **Roundness** [Fig. T4].

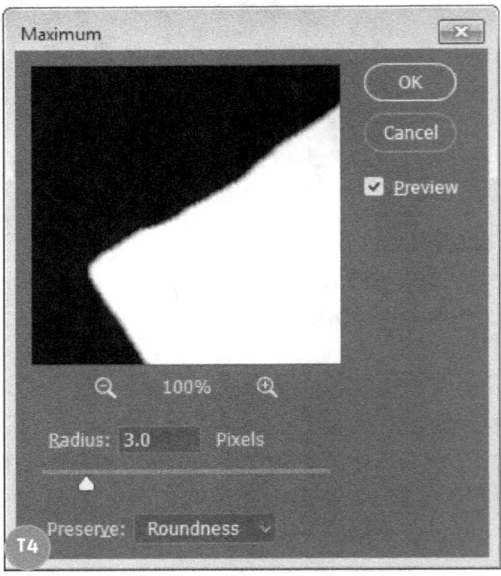

 What just happened?
By specifying a value of **3** for the **Radius** option, we have expanded the white area of the mask to cover the blue haloing.

The **Roundness** option favors the roundness instead of squareness as we expand or shrink the mask using the **Radius** option.

Tutorial 3: Creating Tileable Seamless Texture

Here, we will learn to create a tileable seamless texture in Photoshop [see Figure T1]. This technique is very useful and often used by texturing/digital artists if they have to repeat a texture or pattern. In this example, we will use the **Offset** filter and some Photoshop techniques.

The following table summarizes the tutorial:

Table T3	
Flow: *The following sequence will be used in this tutorial:* *1. Create a new Photoshop document. 2. Open the **grungeMetal.jpg** file. 3. Use the **Offset** filter to create the tileable seamless texture. 4. Use the **Clone** and **Brush** tools to add details.*	
Keywords: *Offset, Clone Stamp, and Brush*	
Difficulty level	Intermediate
Estimated time to complete	45 Minutes
Topics	• Getting Started • Creating the Seamless Texture
Resources folder	**chapter-f3**
Final tutorial file	**f3-tut3-finish.psd**

Getting Started

Open **grungeMetal.jpg**. In order to create a tileable texture, first we will make the texture [that you want to make seamless] square. Pick the **Crop** tool from **Tool Box** and then right-click on the canvas, choose **1x1 [Square]** from the popup menu that appears [see Figure T2]. Press **Enter** to commit the changes.

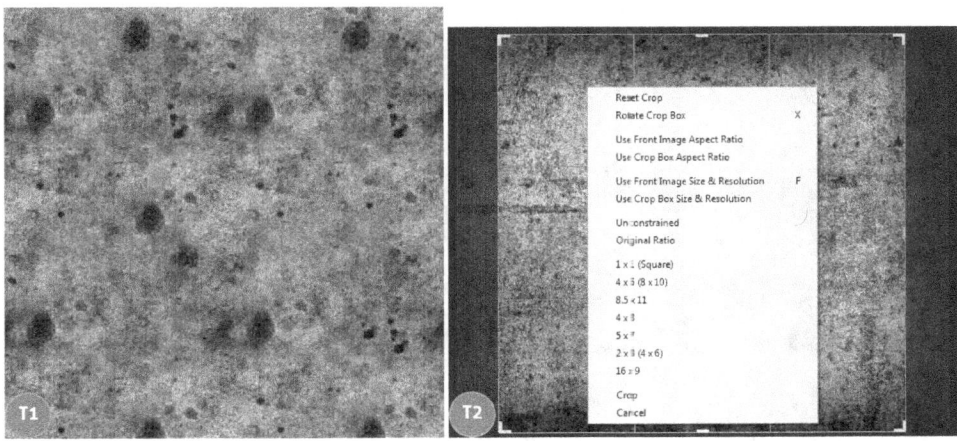

? *What Crop tool does?*
*The **Crop** tool allows you to remove unwanted portions of an image. It also gives you ability to straighten the images. The **Crop** tool is non-destructive tool meaning you can retain the cropped pixels to optimize the crop boundaries later. When you perform a crop on an image, Photoshop gives you real-time feedback to visualize the final result.*

Creating the Seamless Texture
Follow the steps given next:

1. Choose **Image Size** from the **Image** menu. In the **Image Size** dialog box that appears, set **Width** and **Height** to **496** pixels and then click **OK**. Save the Photoshop document as **f3-tut-finish.psd**.

   Tip: Document Size
   *The reason we have changed size from **497** to **496** is that we want an even number [divisible by **2**] here because the **Offset** filter that we will apply later does not accept decimal values.*

   What next?
   Now, let's get rid of the lines or scratches from the texture [see left image in Figure T3]. The reason we want to get rid of those scratches is that they might look odd when texture is tiled.

2. Pick **Clone Stamp Tool** from **Tool Box**. Choose a noise brush [see Figure T4] for **Clone Stamp Tool** and then get rid of these scratches [see right image in Figure T3].

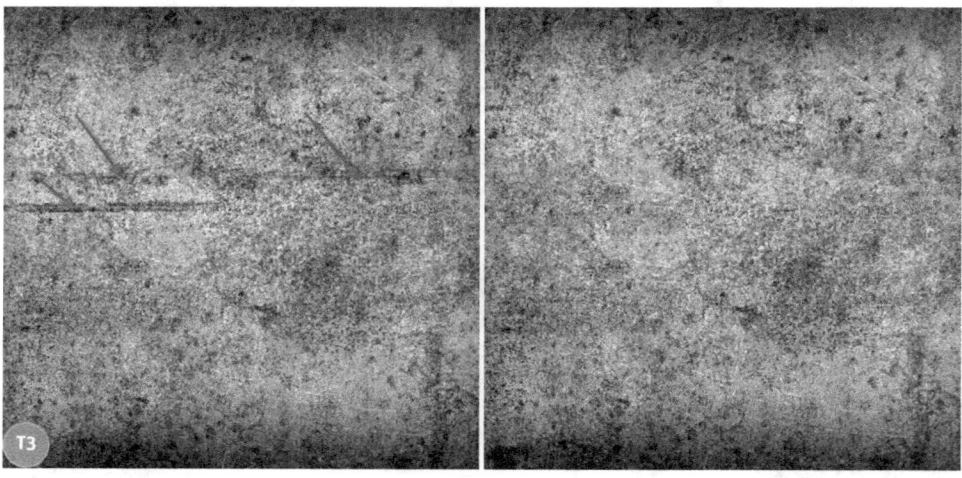

   What Clone Stamp Tool does?
   ***Clone Stamp Tool** allows you to duplicate objects or remove a defect in an image. You can use this tool to paint one part of an image to another part of the same image. You can also paint contents of one layer to another layer. This tool also allows you to set a brush tip. Now, let's add some more details to the texture.*

3. Open **oilTexture.jpg** and place it on the **f3-tut3-finish.psd's** canvas [see Figure T5]. Set **Blending Mode** to **Multiply** for the oil texture.

4. Add a **Levels** adjustment layer and clip it to the oil texture layer. Adjust the levels [see Figure T6]. Ensure the oil texture layer is selected and then click the **Add layer mask** button from the **Layers** panel. Set the foreground color to black and pick a noise brush. Now, paint black on the mask to get rid of the seams and unwanted area [see Figure T7].

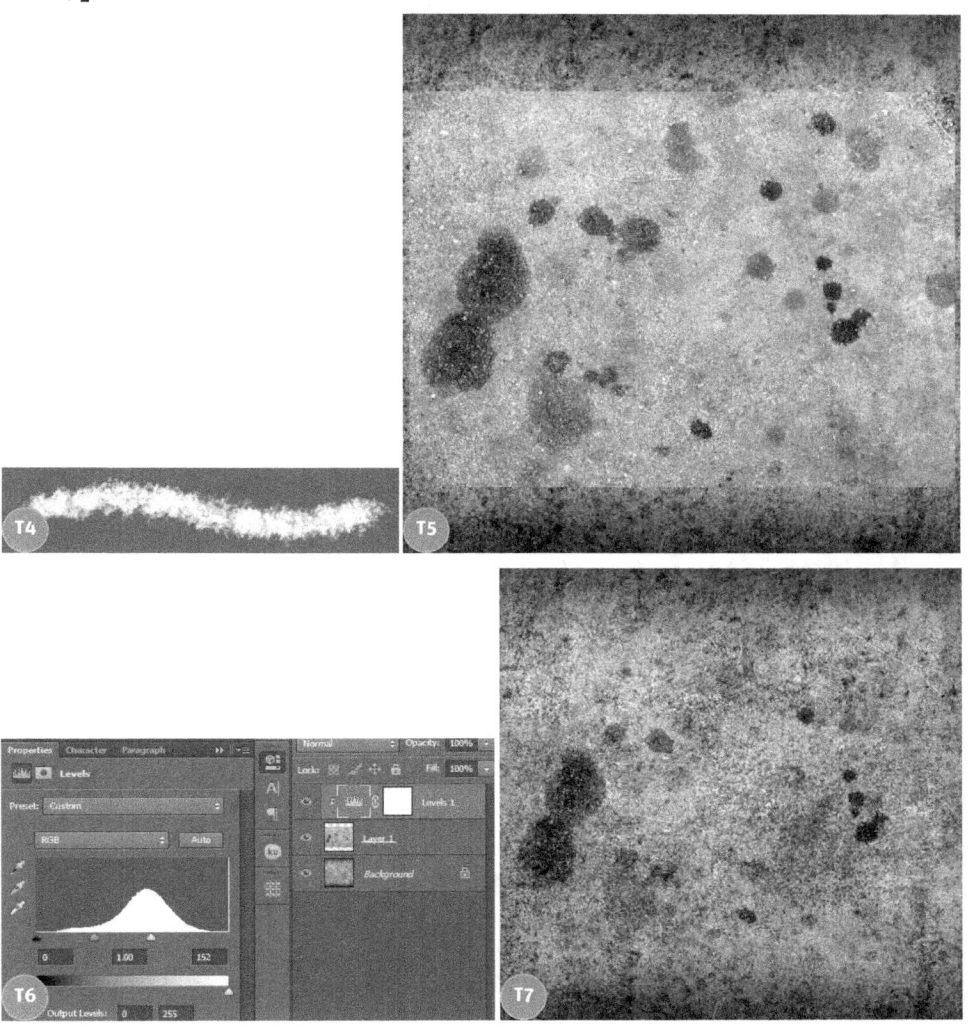

5. Press **Ctrl+A** to select all pixels and then choose **Copy Special | Copy Merged** from the **Edit** menu. Press **Ctrl+V** to paste the data. Ensure the layer is at the top of the stack in the **Layers** panel. Rename layer as **Base**.

6. Press **Ctrl+J** to duplicate the layer and then rename the layer as **Base1**. Choose **Other → Offset** from the **Filter** menu. In the **Offset** dialog that appears, set the parameters as shown in Figure T8 and then click **OK** [see Figure T9].

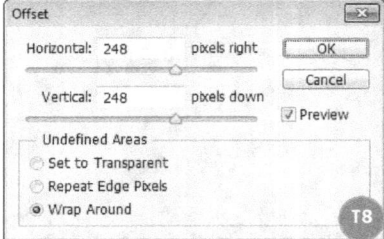
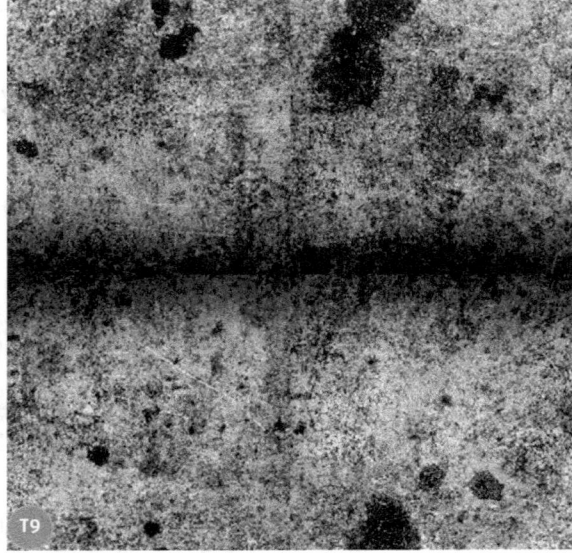

T8   T9

Note: Offset Command
We have used the value **248** pixels for **Horizontal** and **Vertical** because it's half the value of **496**, the **50%** of the original size. The **Wrap Around** feature fills the undefined space with content from the opposite edge of the image.

7. Ensure the **Base1** layer is selected in the **Layers** panel. Click the **Add layer mask** button to add a layer mask. Ensure the **Foreground Color** is set to **Black** and then pick a noise brush. Using the **Brush** tool, paint on the seams to get rid of them. When you paint black, you reveal the layer underneath [see Figure T10].

   Tip: Adding randomness to the texture
   Paint on some other areas [not just the seams] to get some randomness in the texture. You can add more randomness by cloning the some area using **Clone Stamp Tool**. You can also use **Healing Brush Tool** to clone some areas. This tool allows you to preserve the luminosity of the pixels.

8. Choose **Flatten Image** from the **Layer** menu and then unlock the **Background** layer. Choose **Canvas Size** from the **Image** menu. In the **New Size** section of the **Canvas Size** dialog that appears, set the values as shown in Figure T11 and click **OK**.

9. Pick **Move Tool** from the **Tool Box** and then **Alt+drag** layer on the canvas. Press **Shift** to snap the movement [see Figure T12]. Similarly, create two more copies [see Figure T13]. Select all layers in the **Layers** panel and press **Ctrl+E** to merge all layers.

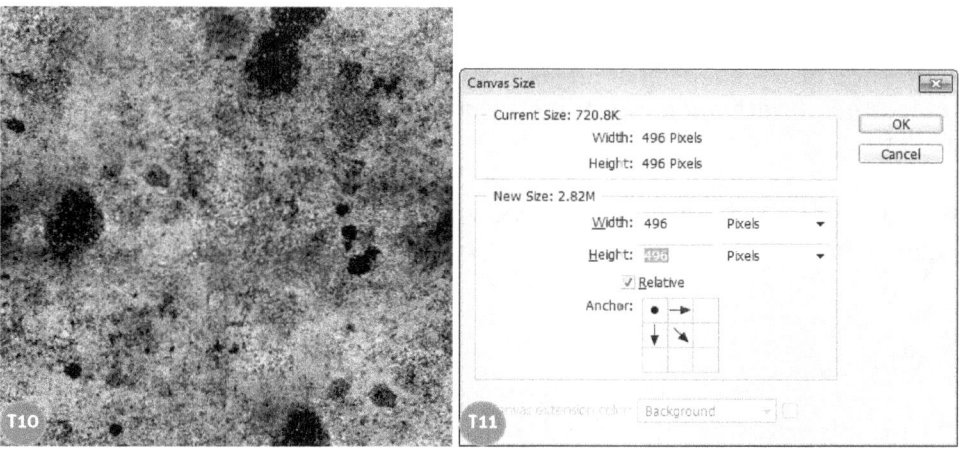

> *Tip: Order of the layers*
> Create and place layers in clockwise direction [see Figure T13].

> *Note: Flatten Image*
> The **Flatten Image** command reduces the file size by merging all visible layers. Any remaining transparent area is filled with white color.

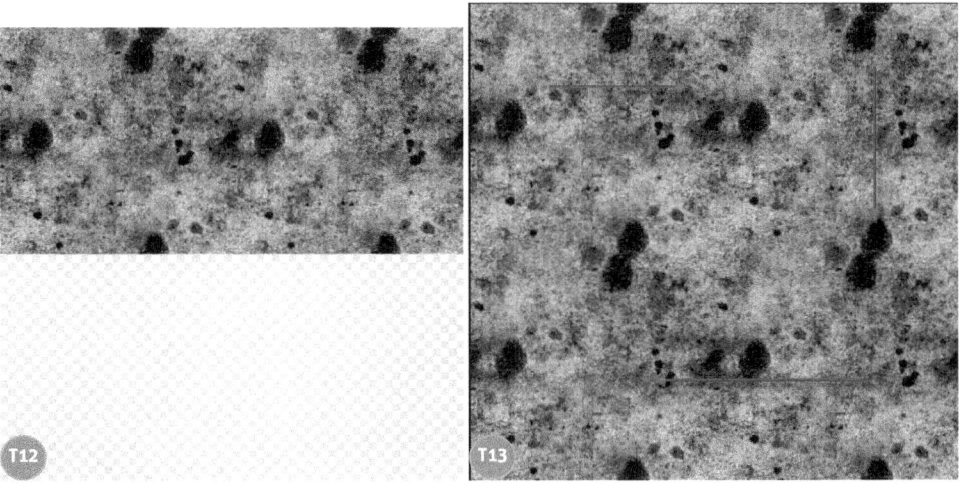

Photoshop CC 2017

Caution: Flatten Image
When you use this command, the images are merged permanently. You cannot revert to the unflattened state.

Caution: Flatten Image
Photoshop also flattens the images, if you switch between the color modes. Therefore, I recommend that you make a backup of your document before you switch the color modes.

If you find some seams in the image or if you want to break the symmetry, do not hesitate in using **Clone Stamp Tool**.

Summary
In this chapter:

- 3 Tutorials covering filters from the **Others** category.
- Covers the following filters: **High Pass**, **Maximum**, and **Offset**

IN THIS CHAPTER:

- 10 Tutorials covering background design creation techniques
- Covers the following filters: **Difference Clouds, Patchwork, Motion Blur, Trace Contour, Halftone Pattern, Lens Flare, Wave, Chrome, Plaster, Twirl, Fibers, Water Paper, Emboss, Clouds, Radial Blur, Sprayed Strokes,** and **Sketch**

Chapter F4

Creating Background Designs

In this chapter, we will create background designs using filters.

Tutorials

Before you start the tutorials, create a folder with the name **chapter-f4**. We'll use this folder to host all the tutorial files and other resources.

Tutorial 1: Creating a Background Design - 1

In this tutorial, we will create a background design made of stripes as shown in Fig. T1. The following table summarizes the tutorial:

Table T1	
Flow: The following sequence will be used in this tutorial: *1. Create a new Photoshop document. 2. Use the **Difference Clouds, Patchwork**, and **Motion Blur** filters to create the design.*	
Keywords: Difference Clouds, Patchwork, and Motion Blur	
Difficulty level	Beginner
Topics	• Getting Started • Creating the Design
Estimated time to complete	15 Minutes
Resources folder	**chapter-f4**
Final tutorial file	**f4_tut1_finish.psd**

Getting Started

Create a new **1000x1000 PX** Photoshop document and then set the **Foreground** and **Background** colors as follows: **#995a00** and **#dcab4c**. Covert the **Background** layer to a smart object.

Creating the Design

Follow the steps given next:

1. Choose **Render | Difference Clouds** from the **Filter** menu [Fig. T2]. Choose **Filter Gallery | Texture | Patchwork** from the **Filter** menu and then set **Square Size** to **5** and **Relief** to **25**. Click **OK** [Fig. T3].

   > *Note: Patchwork Filter*
   > *It breaks the image into squares. These squares are filled with the predominant color in that area of the image. It randomly reduces or increases the tile depth to make highlights and shadows.*

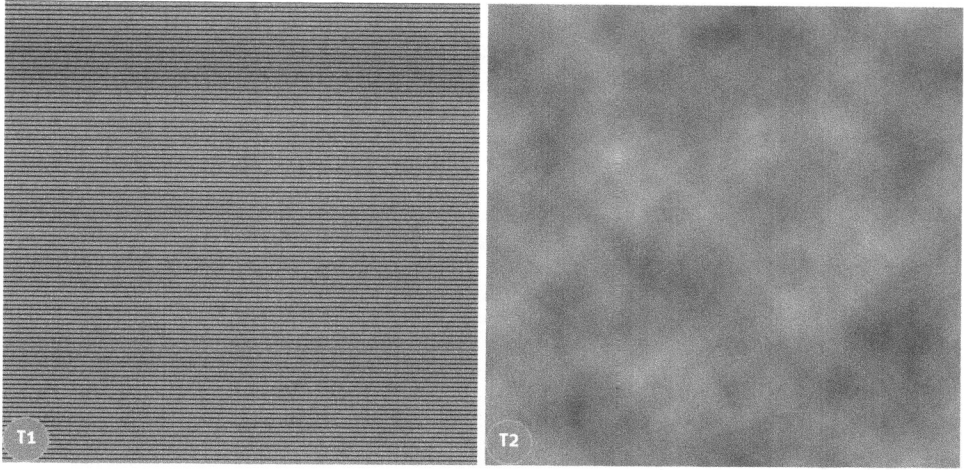

2. Choose **Blur | Motion Blur** from the **Filter** menu. In the **Motion Blur** dialog box that opens, set **Angle** to **0, Distance** to **2000** and then click **OK** [Fig. T4].

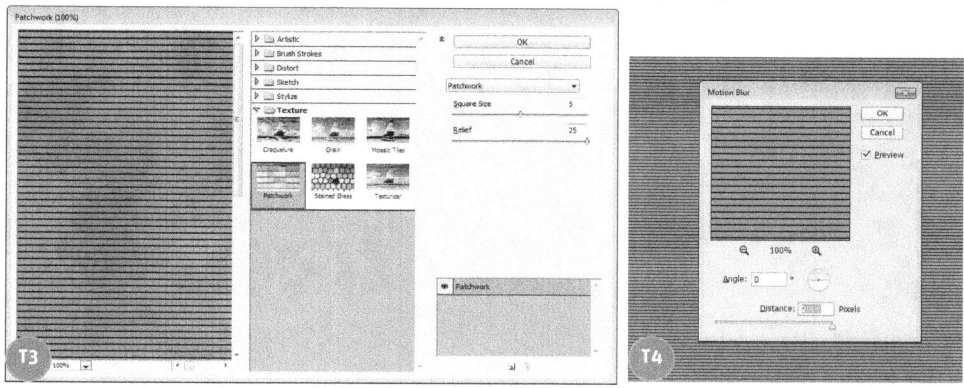

Note: Motion Blur Filter
*This filter is used to blur pixels in the specified direction. You can specify the range from **-360** degrees to **+360** degrees.*

Tutorial 2: Creating a Background Design - 2

In this tutorial, we will create an abstract design, Fig. T1. The following table summarizes the tutorial:

Table T2
Flow: The following sequence will be used in this tutorial:
*1. Create a new Photoshop document. 2. Use the **Trace Contour** filter to create the design.*
Keywords: *Trace Contour, Motion Blur, and Twirl*

Table T2	
Difficulty level	Beginner
Topics	• Getting Started • Creating the Design
Estimated time to complete	20 Minutes
Resources folder	chapter-f4
Final tutorial file	f4_tut2_finish.psd

Getting Started

Create a new **1000x1000 PX** Photoshop document and then set the **Foreground Color** to **#00aeef**. Unlock the **Background** layer and fill it with the **Foreground** color. Apply the **Satin** layer style and set the values shown in Fig. T2. Fig. T3 shows the result.

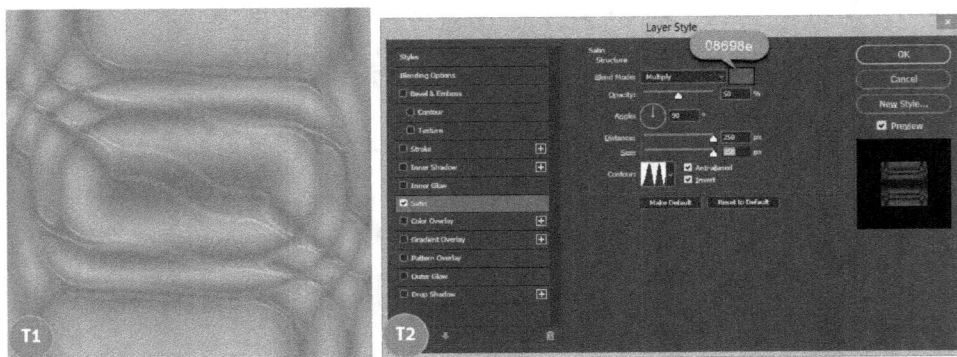

Creating the Design

Follow the steps given next:

1. Press **Ctrl+J** to duplicate the layer. RMB click on the layer's name in the **Layers** panel and then choose **Rasterize Layer Style** from the popup menu. Choose **Stylize | Trace Contour** from the **Filter** menu. In the **Trace Contour** dialog box that opens, set **Level** to **128**, **Edge** to **Upper**, and then click **OK** [Fig. T4].

   > *Note: Trace Contour Filter*
   > *The **Trace Contour** filter creates a contour map like effect. It finds transitions between the major brightness areas and then outlines those areas for each color channel.*

2. Choose **Blur | Motion Blur** from the **Filter** menu. In the **Motion Blur** dialog box that opens, set **Angle** to **-40**, **Distance** to **23**, and then click **OK** [Fig. T5]. Set **Blending Mode** to **Divide** for the selected layer. Choose **Distort | Twirl** from the **Filter** menu. In the **Twirl** dialog box that appears, set **Angle** to **51** as shown in Fig. T6 and then click **OK**.

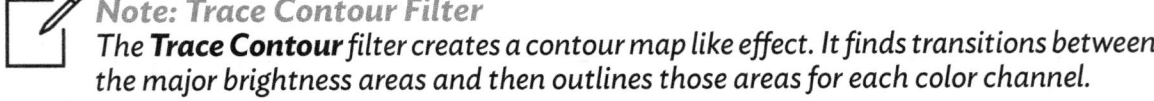

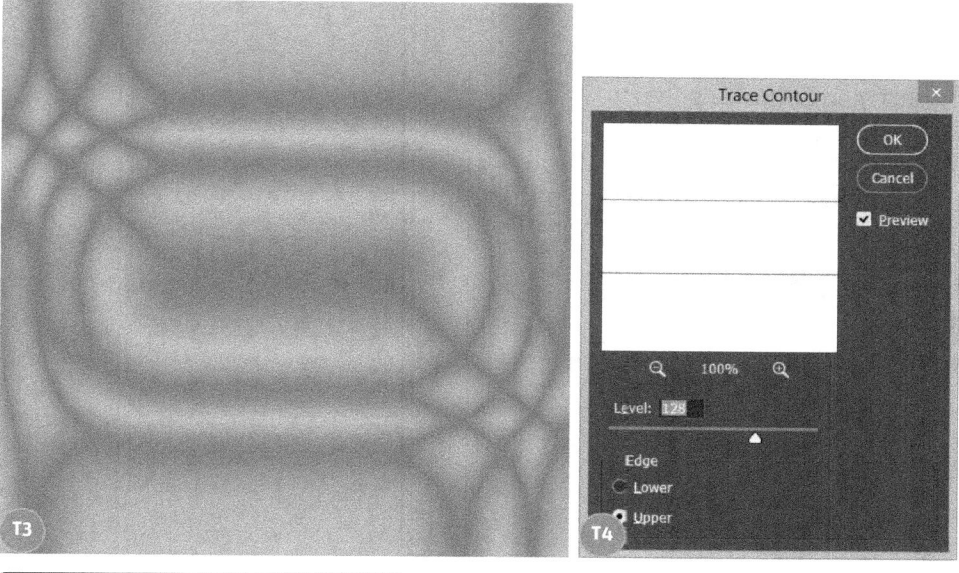

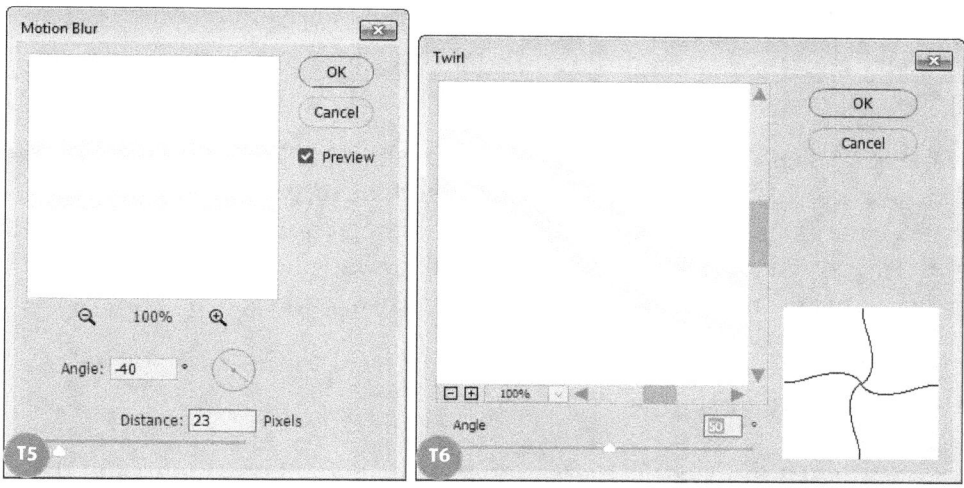

Note: Twirl Filter
This filter rotates a selection. If you specify an angle, it produces a twirl pattern.

Tutorial 3: Creating a Background Design - 3

In this tutorial, we will create a design that looks like a digital circuit board, Fig. T1. The following table summarizes the tutorial:

Table T3	
Flow: *The following sequence will be used in this tutorial:* *1. Create a new Photoshop document. 2. Use the **Trace Contour**, **Water Paper**, and **Halftone Pattern** filters to create the design.*	
Keywords: *Trace Contour, Water Paper, and Halftone Pattern*	
Difficulty level	Intermediate
Estimated time to complete	20 Minutes
Topics	• Getting Started • Creating the Design
Resources folder	chapter-f4
Final tutorial file	f4_tut3_finish.psd

Getting Started

Create a new **1000x1000 PX** document with the white background. Press **D** to reset the foreground and background layers. Choose **Convert for Smart Filters** from the **Filter** menu. On doing so, a message box appears. Click **OK** and then choose **Noise | Add Noise** from the **Filter** menu to open the **Add Noise** dialog box. In this dialog box, ensure the **Monochromatic** switch is on. Set **Amount** to **20**, **Distribution** to **Gaussian**, and then click **OK**.

Creating the Texture

Follow the steps given next:

1. Choose **Filter Gallery | Sketch | Halftone Pattern** from the **Filter** menu and then set **Size** to **2** and **Contrast** to **4**. Ensure **Dot** is selected as **Pattern Type** and then click **OK** [Fig. T2].

2. Choose **Filter Gallery | Sketch | Water Paper** from the **Filter** menu and then set **Fiber Length** to **45**, **Brightness** to **76**, and **Contrast** to **71**. Click **OK** [Fig. T3]. Choose **Stylize | Trace Contour** from the **Filter** menu. In the **Trace Contour** dialog box that opens, set **Level** to **155**, **Edge** to **Upper**, and then click **OK** [Fig. T4].

3. Press **Ctrl+A** to select all pixels and then choose **Copy Special | Copy Merged** from the **Edit** menu. Now, press **Ctrl+V**. Create a new layer and place it below **Layer 1**. Fill the

layer with the **#58712b** color. Ensure **Layer 1** is selected in the **Layers** panel and then press **Ctrl+I** to invert the layer. Also, set **Blending Mode** to **Screen**.

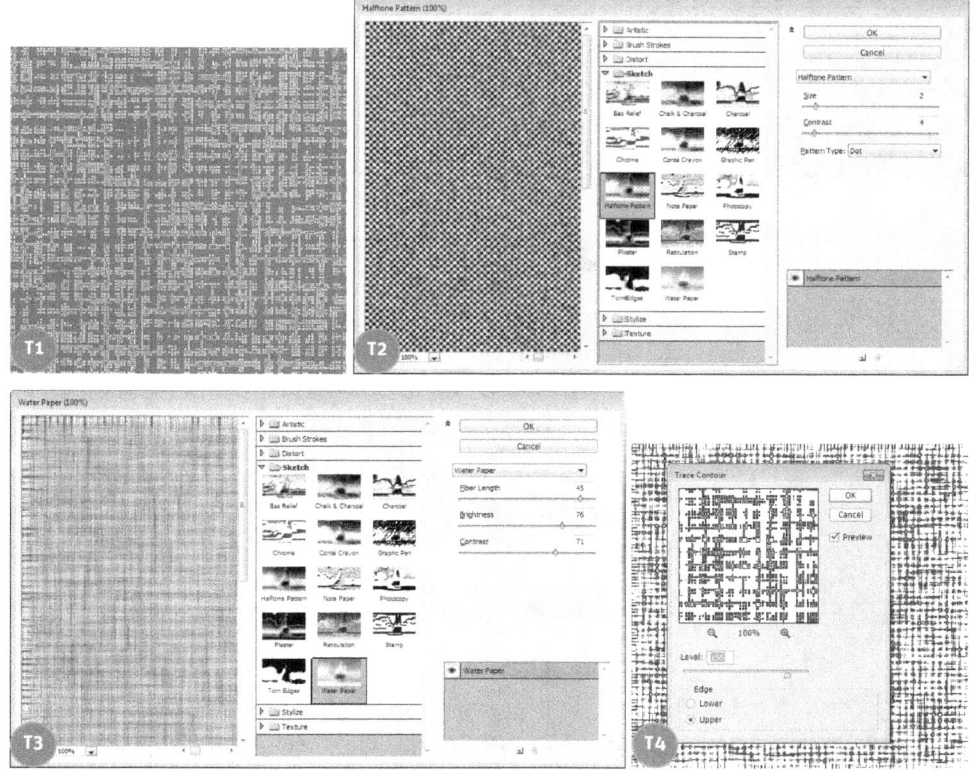

Tutorial 4: Creating a Background Design - 4

In this tutorial, we will create a line art design, Fig. T1. The following table summarizes the tutorial:

Table T4	
Flow: *The following sequence will be used in this tutorial:*	
1. Open the image. 2. Use the **Motion Blur, Emboss,** and **Trace Contour** filters to create the design.	
Keywords: *Motion Blur, Emboss, and Trace Contour*	
Difficulty level	Intermediate
Estimated time to complete	30 Minutes
Topics	• Getting Started • Creating the Design

Photoshop CC 2017

Table T4	
Resources folder	chapter-f4
Final tutorial file	f4_tut4_finish.psd

Getting Started
Open **crumpledPaper.psd**. Choose **Stylize | Emboss** from the **Filter** menu. In the **Emboss** dialog box that appears, set **Angle** to **-13**, **Height** to **100**, and **Amount** to **500** [Fig. T2]. Click **OK**.

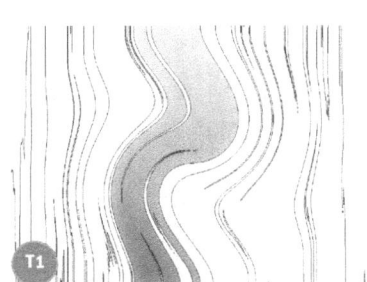
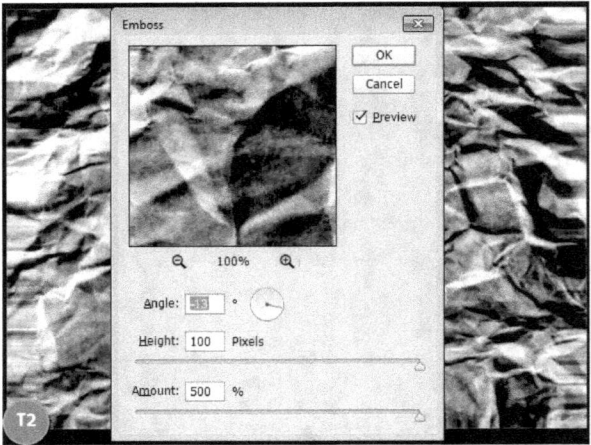

Note: Emboss Filter
This filter makes an image raised or stamped. It converts fill color of the image to gray and traces the edges with the original fill color.

 Tip: Fade Command
If you want to retain the color detailing, use the **Fade** command after applying the **Emboss** filter.

Creating the Design
Follow these steps:

1. Choose **Blur | Motion Blur** from the **Filter** menu. In the **Motion Blur** dialog box that opens, set **Angle** to **90**, **Distance** to **2000**, and then click **OK** [Fig. T3]. Choose **Distort | Twirl** from the **Filter** menu. In the **Twirl** dialog box that appears, set **Angle** to **93** [Fig. T4] and then click **OK**.

2. Choose **Stylize | Trace Contour** from the **Filter** menu. In the **Trace Contour** dialog box that opens, set **Level** to **132**, **Edge** to **Upper**, and then click **OK** [Fig. T5]. Using the **Magic Wand Tool**, make a selection, refer Fig. T6.

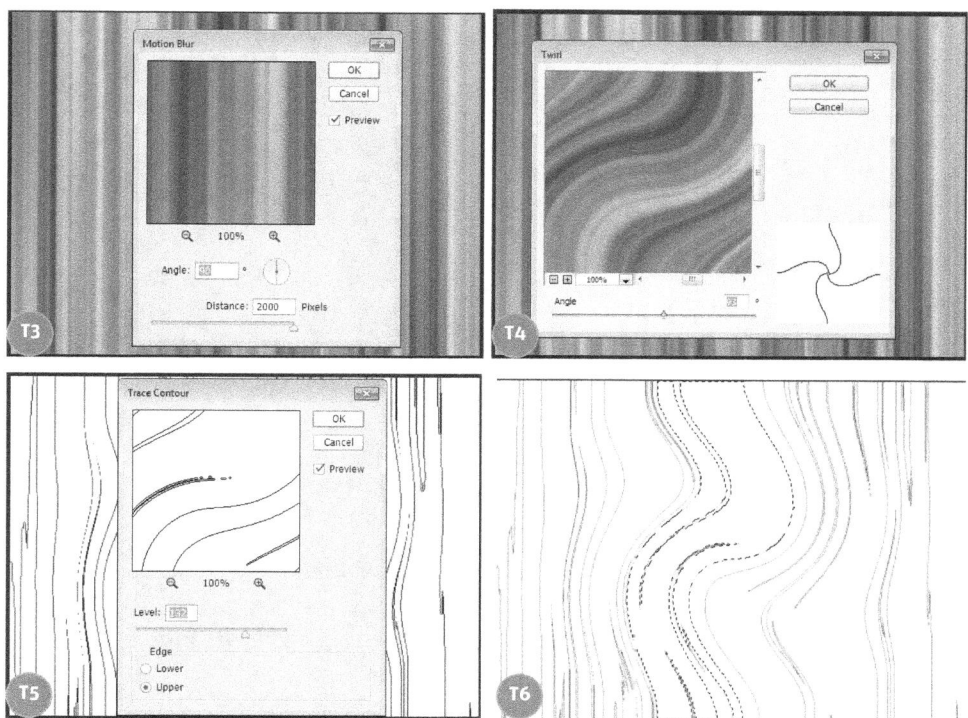

3. Create a new layer and fill it with the black color [Fig. T7]. Apply **Gradient Overlay** and **Inner Shadow** layer styles [Figs. T8 and T9] for settings.

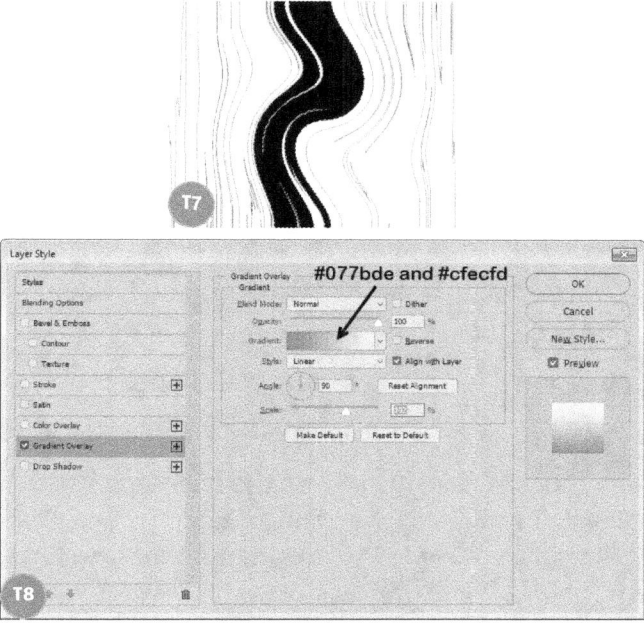

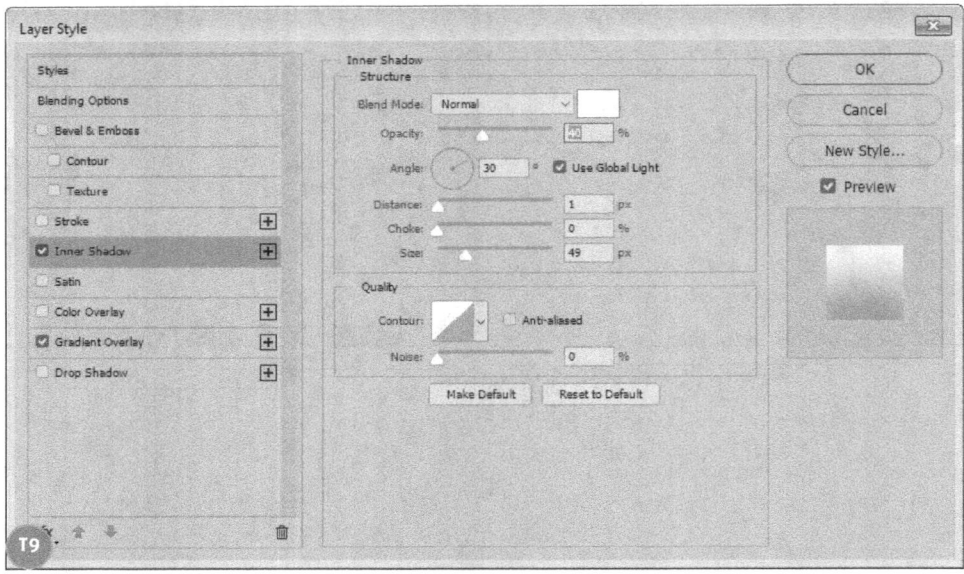

Tutorial 5: Creating a Background Design - 5

In this tutorial, we will create a background design, as shown in Fig. T1. The following table summarizes the tutorial:

Table T5	
Flow: The following sequence will be used in this tutorial: 1. Open the **carinaNebula.jpg** file. 2. Use the **Calculations** command and the **Lens Flare, Emboss,** and **Wave** filter to create the effect.	
Keywords: Calculations, Lens Flare, Emboss, and Wave	
Difficulty level	Intermediate
Estimated time to complete	25 Minutes
Topics	• Getting Started • Creating the Design
Resources folder	**chapter-f4**
Final tutorial file	**f4_tut5_finish.psd**

Getting Started

Open **carinaNebula.jpg**. Choose **Calculations** from the **Image** menu. In the **Calculations** dialog box that opens, set **Channel** to **Blue** in the **Source 1** section. Set **Channel** to **Red** from the **Source 2** section. Set **Blending** to **Overlay**. Also, ensure that **New Channel** is selected from the **Result** drop-down [Fig. T2]. Click **OK**.

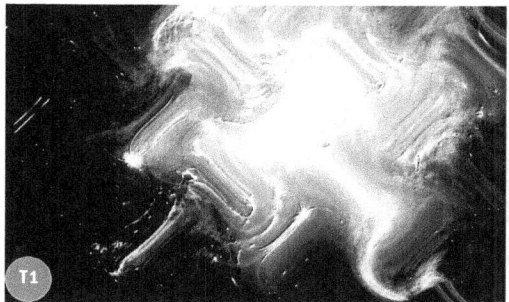 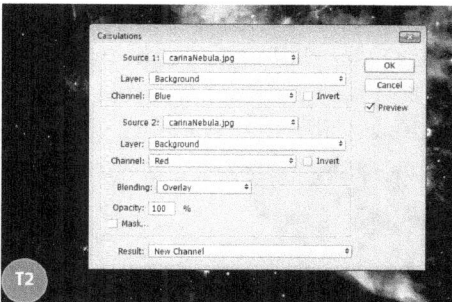

> **Note: Calculations Command**
> The **Calculations** command allows you to blend two individual channels from one or more source images. You can apply results to a new image, new selection, or selection in the active image.

> **Warning: Calculations Command**
> If you are using two source images, the images must have the same pixel dimensions.

Creating the Design
Follow the steps given next:

1. Switch to the **Channels** panel. Ensure that the **Alpha 1** channel is selected [Fig. T3]. Press **Ctrl+A** and then **Ctrl+C** to copy the channel data. Now, select the **RGB** channel layer. Switch back to the **Layers** panel and then press **Ctrl+V** to paste the data [Fig. T4].

2. Set the **Foreground** and **Background** colors to **#8f2c00** and **#b93904**, respectively. Create a new layer and place it under the pasted layer and then using **Gradient Tool** fill the layer. Set **Blending Mode** to **Linear Light** for the **Layer 1** [Fig. T5].

3. Ensure **Layer 1** is selected and then choose **Lens Flare** from the **Filter | Render** menu. In the **Lens Flare** dialog box that opens, place the hotspot as shown in Fig. T6, and then click **OK**. Fig. T7 shows the result. Choose **Distort | Wave** from the **Filter** menu. In the **Wave** dialog box that appears, set the values, shown in Fig. T8 and then click **OK**.

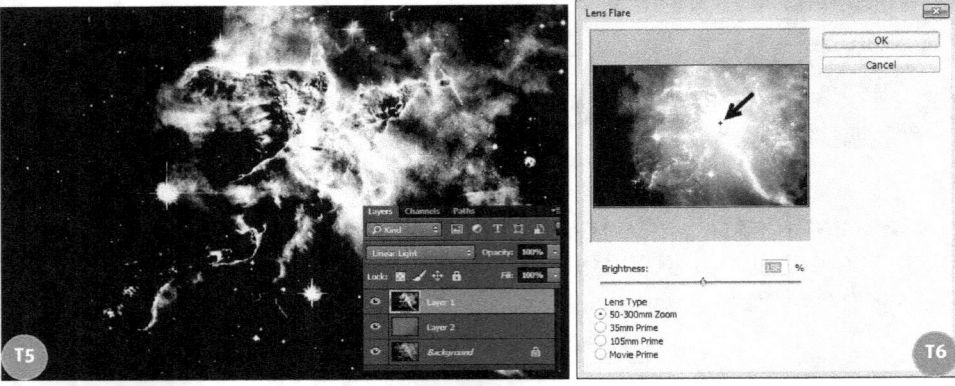

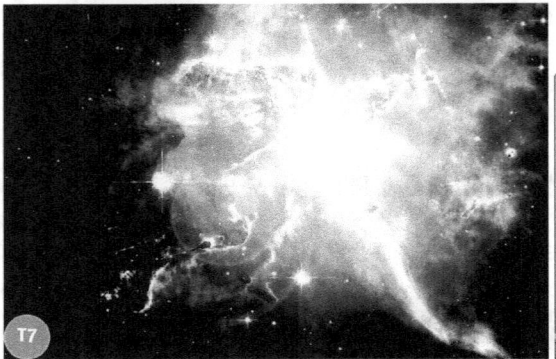

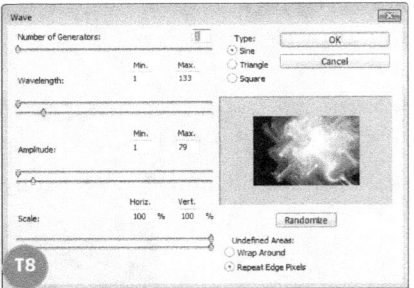

 Note: Lens Flare
The **Lens Flare** filter allows you to simulate the refraction caused by shining a bright light into a camera lens.

Note: Wave Filter
This filter is like the **Ripple** filter but it provides better control. It creates an undulating pattern on a selection.

4. Press **Ctrl+J** to duplicate **Layer 1** and then choose **Stylize | Emboss** from the **Filter** menu. In the **Emboss** dialog box that appears, set **Angle** to **135**, **Height** to **3**, and **Amount** to **100** [Fig. T9]. Click **OK**.

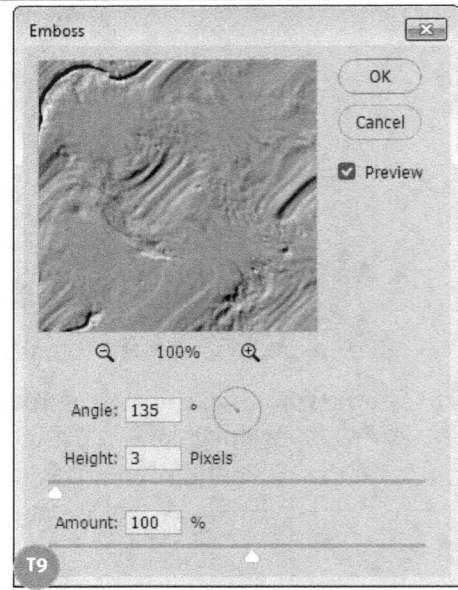

Tutorial 6: Creating a Background Design - 6

In this tutorial, we will create a metallic background design, as shown in Fig. T1. The following table summarizes the tutorial:

Table T6	
Flow: *The following sequence will be used in this tutorial:* *1. Create a new Photoshop document. 2. Use the **Lens Flare**, **Chrome**, **Polar Coordinates**, and **Wave** filters to create the design.*	
Keywords: *Lens Flare, Polar Coordinates, Chrome, and Wave*	
Difficulty level	Intermediate
Estimated time to complete	30 Minutes
Topics	• Getting Started • Creating the Design
Resources folder	**chapter-f4**
Final tutorial file	**f4_tut6_finish.psd**

Getting Started

Create a new **1000x1000 PX** Photoshop document and fill it with black. Create a new layer and fill it with black as well. Choose **Lens Flare** from the **Filter | Render** menu. Set the values in the **Lens Flare** dialog box that opens, as shown in Fig. T2 and then click **OK**.

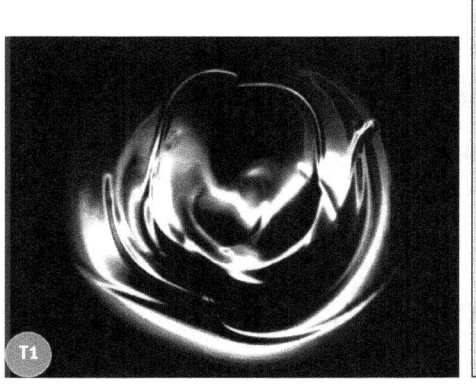
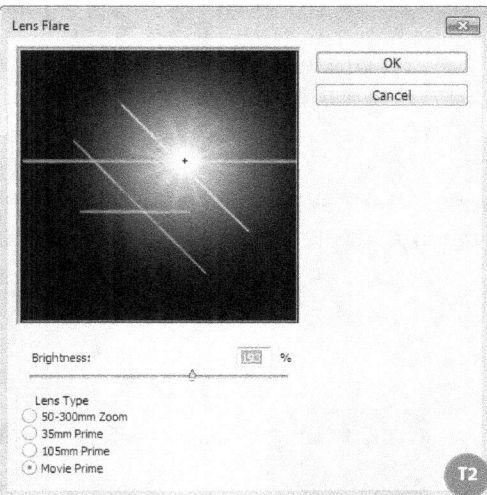

Creating the Design

Follow the steps given next:

1. Press **Ctrl+J** to create a duplicate layer and then choose **Transform | Flip Horizontal** from the **Edit** menu. Set **Blending Mode** to **Screen** [Fig. T3]. Merge the upper two layers. Choose **Distort | Wave** from the **Filter** menu. In the **Wave** dialog box that appears, set the values, shown in Fig. T4 and then click **OK**.

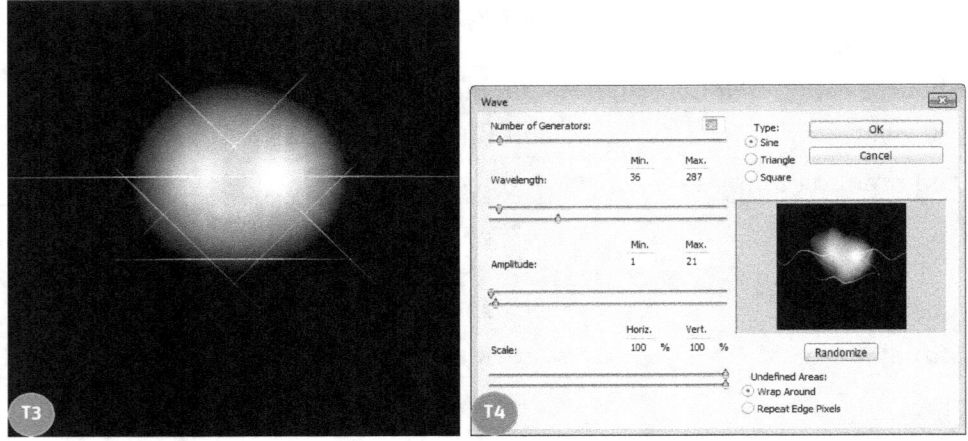

2. Choose **Distort | Polar Coordinates** from the **Filter** menu. In the **Polar Coordinates** dialog box that appears, select **Rectangular to Polar** and then click **OK** [Fig. T5].

> *Note: Polar Coordinates Filter*
> *This filter can be used to create a cylinder anamorphosis, a form of art that was popular in the 18th century. It converts a selection from rectangular to polar coordinates and visa-versa.*

3. Choose **Filter Gallery | Sketch | Chrome** from the **Filter** menu and then set **Detail** to **5** and **Smoothness** to **7**. Click **OK** [Fig. T6].

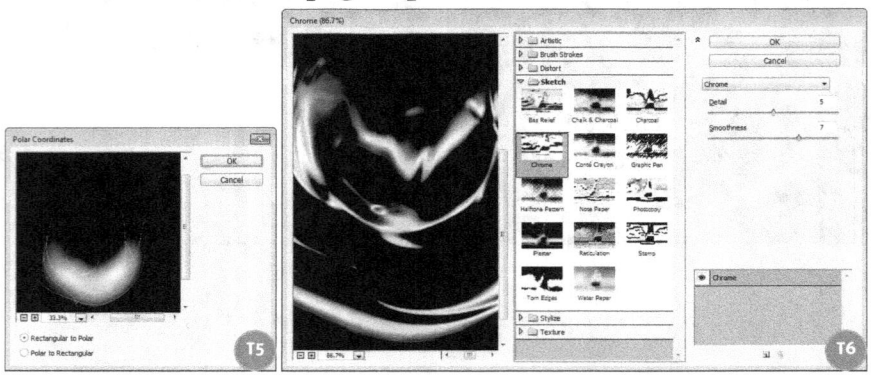

Note: *Chrome Filter*
This filter allows you to render the image as if it had a polished chrome surface. The areas with highlights are raised whereas areas with shadows appear lower.

 Tip: *Chrome Filter*
*If you are using this filter, use the **Levels** adjustment to add more contrast to the image.*

4. Add a **Curves** adjustment layer and adjust the curve [Fig. T7].

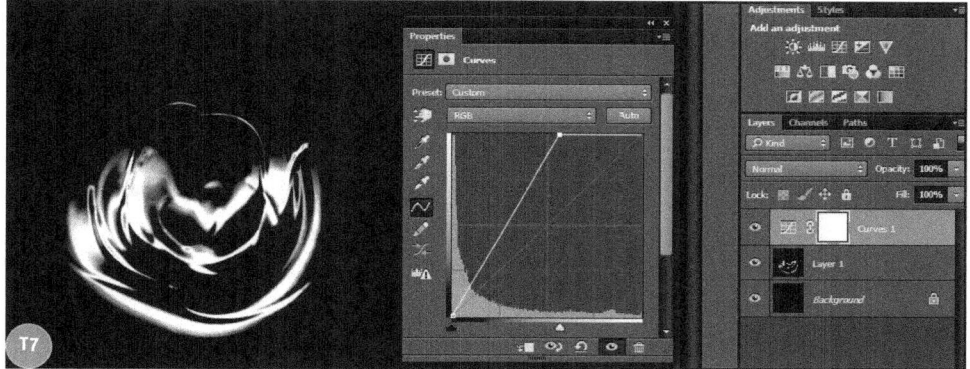

5. Add a **Hue and Saturation** adjustment layer and check the **Colorize** check box in the **Properties** panel. Adjust the **Hue** slider to give the design some color [Fig. T8].

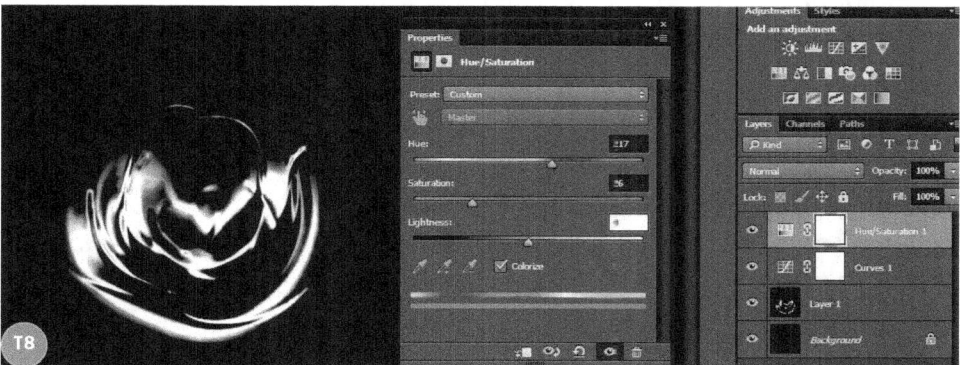

Tutorial 7: Creating a Background Design - 7

In this tutorial, we will create a background design, as shown in Fig. T1. The following table summarizes the tutorial:

Table T7	
Flow: The following sequence will be used in this tutorial: 1. Create a new Photoshop document. 2. Use the **Chrome, Plaster, Clouds,** and **Wave** filters to create the texture.	
Keywords: Chrome, Plaster, Clouds, and Wave	
Difficulty level	Intermediate
Estimated time to complete	20 Minutes
Topics	• Getting Started • Creating the Design
Resources folder	chapter-f4
Final tutorial file	f4_tut7_finish.psd

Getting Started

Create a new **1000x1000** px Photoshop document. Press **D** to set the **Foreground** and **Background** colors to default. Choose **Render** | **Clouds** from the **Filter** menu. Unlock the **Background** layer.

Creating the Design

Follow the steps given next:

1. Choose **Filter Gallery** | **Sketch** | **Chrome** from the **Filter** menu and then set **Detail** to **0** and **Smoothness** to **10** [Fig. T2]. Click **New Effect Layer** and click **Sketch** | **Plaster** [Fig. T3] and then click **OK**.

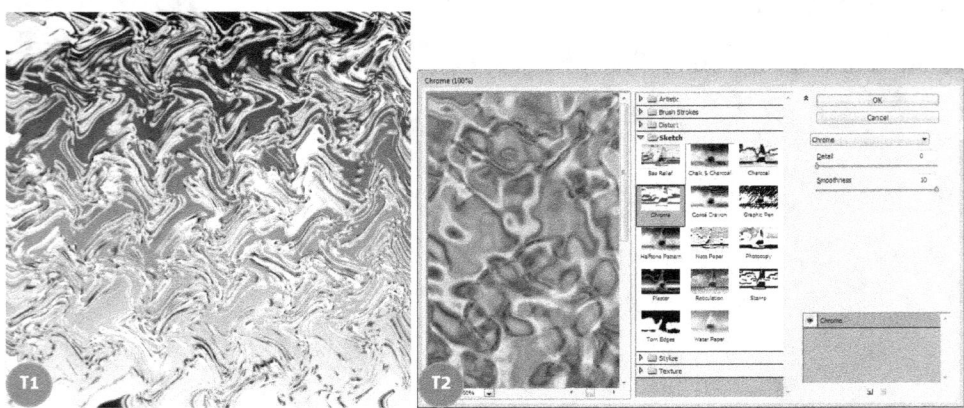

2. Choose **Distort | Wave** from the **Filter** menu. In the **Wave** dialog box that appears, set the values, as shown in Fig. T4 and then click **OK**. Fig. T5 shows the result.

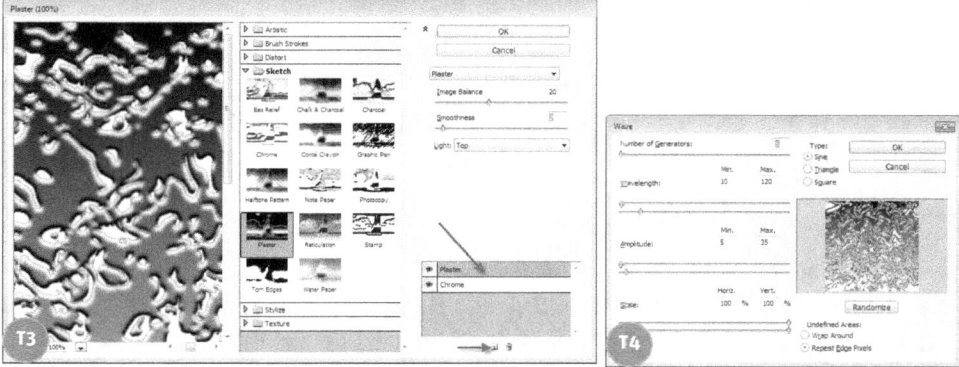

3. Press **Ctrl+J** to create the duplicate of **Layer 0**. Choose **Distort | Wave** from the **Filter** menu. In the **Wave** dialog box that appears, click **Randomize** then click **OK**. Set the blending mode to **Lighten**. Add a **Color Balance** adjustment layer and then set the values as shown in Fig. T6.

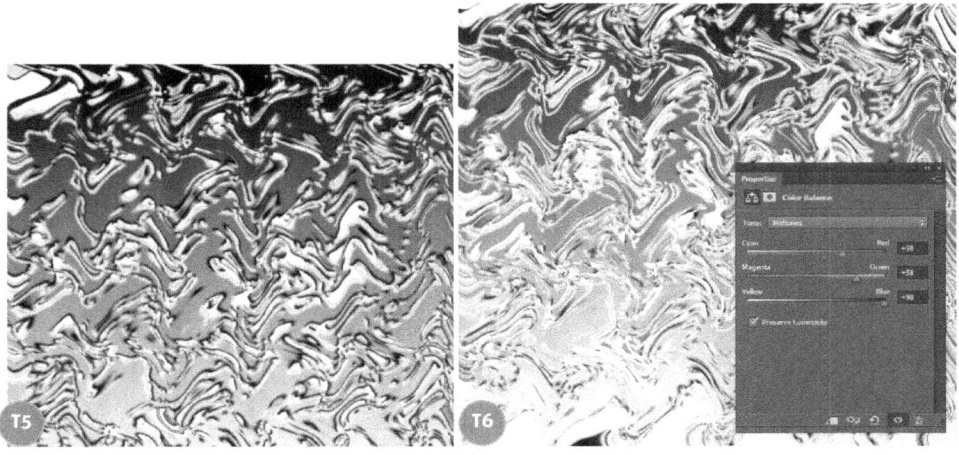

Tutorial 8: Creating a Background Design - 8

In this tutorial, we will create a background design, as shown in Fig. T1. The following table summarizes the tutorial:

Table T8
Flow: *The following sequence will be used in this tutorial:*   *1. Open the Hubble image. 2. Use the **Chrome** and **Wave** filters to create the design.*
Keywords: *Chrome and Wave*

Photoshop CC 2017

Table T8	
Difficulty level	Intermediate
Estimated time to complete	15 Minutes
Topics	• Getting Started • Creating the Design
Resources folder	**chapter-f4**
Final tutorial file	**f4_tut8_finish.psd**

Getting Started

Google the following term: **Stephan's Quintet Hubble**, then download the image. Open the downloaded image in Photoshop. Unlock the **Background** layer. Choose **Filter Gallery | Sketch | Chrome** from the **Filter** menu and then make sure that **Detail** and **Smoothness** is set to **0** and **10**, respectively [Fig. T2].

Creating the Design

Follow the steps given next:

1. Create two copies of **Layer 0** and rename them as **Layer 1** and **Layer 2**. Turn off **Layer 2** and then select **Layer 1**. Choose **Distort | Wave** from the **Filter** menu. In the **Wave** dialog box that appears, accept the default values and then click **OK**. Change blending mode to **Lighten** [Fig. T3].

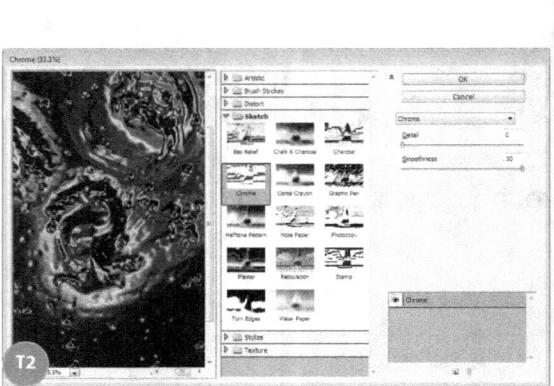
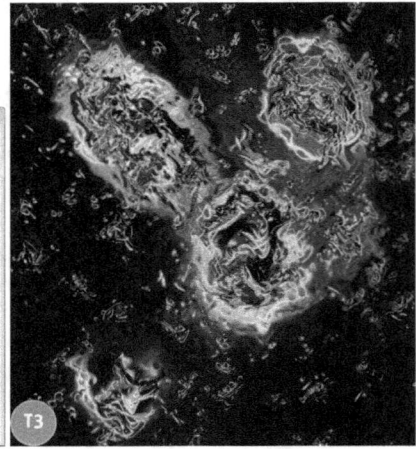

2. Select **Layer 2** and turn it on. Choose **Distort | Wave** from the **Filter** menu. In the **Wave** dialog box that appears, click **Randomize** couple of times to get a different pattern

and then click **OK**. Set blending mode to **Screen**. Merge the layers and then apply the **Extrude** filter to get some interesting results.

Tutorial 9: Creating a Background Design - 9

In this tutorial, we will create a background design, as shown in Fig. T1. The following table summarizes the tutorial:

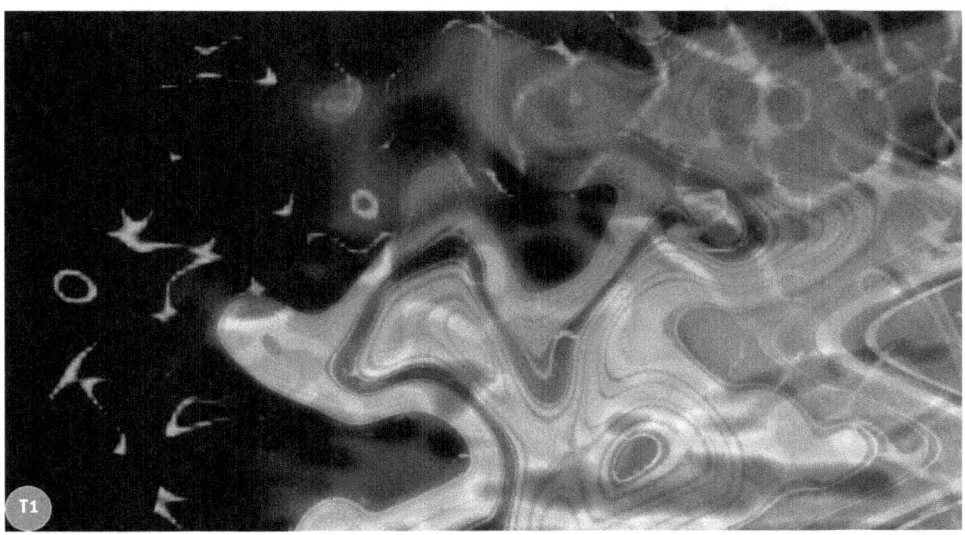

Table T9	
Flow: The following sequence will be used in this tutorial:	
*1. Create a new Photoshop document. 2. Use the **Brush tool**, and the **Motion Blur, Twirl**, and **Wave** filters to create the design.*	
Keywords: Brush, Motion Blur, Twirl, and Wave	
Difficulty level	Intermediate
Estimated time to complete	30 Minutes
Topics	• Getting Started • Creating the Design
Resources folder	chapter-f4
Final tutorial file	f4_tut9_finish.psd

Getting Started

Start a new **1280x720** px document and then fill the background layer with black. Create a new layer. Set the **Foreground** color to white and then choose brush number **74** [**Scattered Maple Leaves**] and paint the strokes [Fig. T2]. Apply the **Color Overlay** style to the **Layer 1** [Fig. T3].

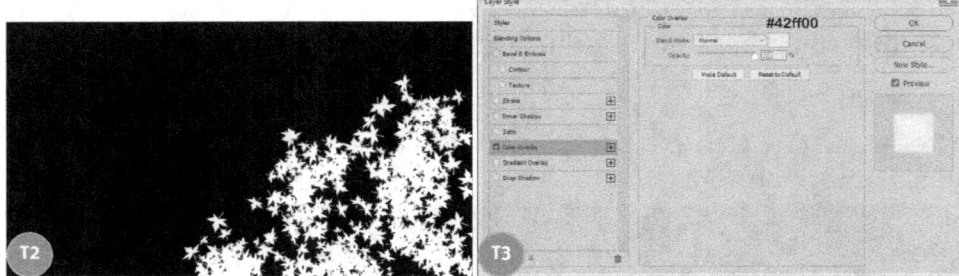

Creating the Design
Follow the steps given next:

1. Press **Ctrl+J** to duplicate **Layer 1** and rename it is **Layer 2**. Select **Layer 2** and choose **Blur | Motion Blur** from the **Filter** menu. In the **Motion Blur** dialog box that appears, set **Angle** to **90** and **Distance** to **2000**. Click **OK** [Fig. T4].

2. Choose **Distort | Twirl** from the **Filter** menu. In the **Twirl** dialog box that appears, set **Angle** to **150** and click **OK** [Fig. T5]. Select **Layer 2** and press **Ctrl+J** to create a duplicate and rename is as **Layer 3**. Select **Layer 2** and **Layer 3** and press **Ctrl+E** to merge them.

3. Select **Layer 1** and then choose **Distort | Twirl** from the **Filter** menu. In the **Twirl** dialog box that appears, set **Angle** to **150** and click **OK**. Choose **Distort | Wave** from the **Filter** menu. In the **Wave** dialog box that appears, set the values as shown in Fig. T6 and then click **OK** [See Fig. T7]. Duplicate **Layer 3** and rename the duplicated layer as **Layer 4**.

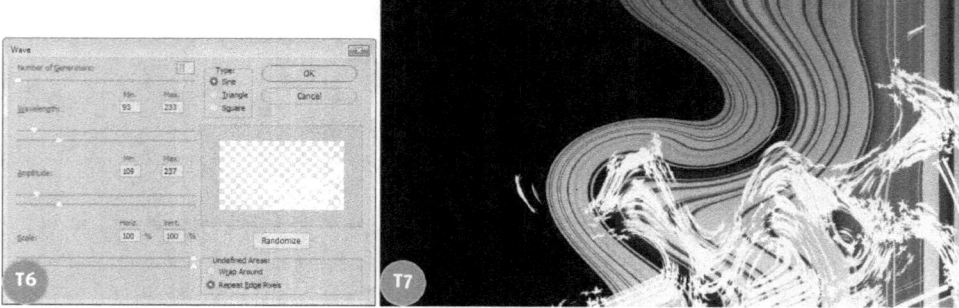

4. Select **Layer 3** and choose **Blur | Gaussian Blur** from the **Filter** menu. In the **Gaussian Blur** dialog box that opens, set **Radius** to **20** and click **OK**.

5. Select **Layer 3** and **Layer 4**. Press **Ctrl+E** to merge the layers. Apply the **Wave** filter to the **Layer 4**. Use the same settings as before [Fig. T8]. Set **Opacity** of **Layer 1** to **20%**. Merge **Layer 1** and **Layer 4**. RMB click on **Layer 4** and choose **Blending Options**. In the **Layer Style** dialog box that appears, click **Styles**. Load **KS Styles** and then click on the second style [Fig. T9]. Click **OK**.

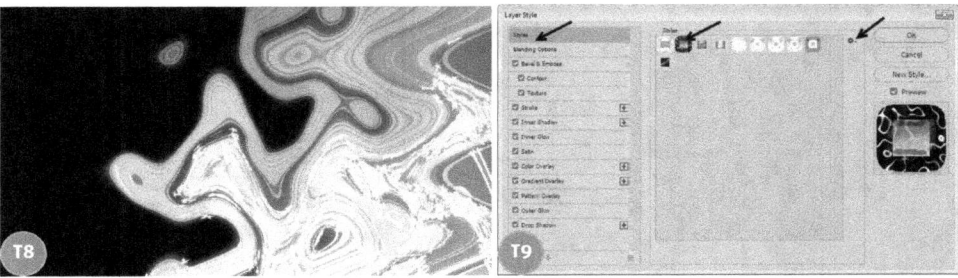

6. Press **Ctrl+A** to select all pixels. Press **Ctrl+Shift+C** to copy the merged pixels and then press **Ctrl+V** to paste them. Select the newly created **Layer 5** and then choose **Blur | Gaussian Blur** from the **Filter** menu. In the **Gaussian Blur** dialog box that opens, set **Radius** to **0.5** and click **OK**.

Tutorial 10: Creating a Background Design - 10

In this tutorial, we will create a background design, as shown in Fig. T1. The following table summarizes the tutorial:

Table T10	
Flow: *The following sequence will be used in this tutorial:* *1. Create a new Photoshop document. 2. Use the* **Fibres, Plaster, Twirl, Sprayed Strokes, Radial Blur,** *and* **Sketch** *filters to create the design.*	
Keywords: *Fibres, Plaster, Twirl, Sprayed Strokes, Radial Blur, and Sketch*	
Difficulty level	Intermediate
Estimated time to complete	20 Minutes
Topics	• Getting Started • Creating the Design
Resources folder	chapter-f4
Final tutorial file	f4_tut10_finish.psd

Getting Started

Create a new **1000x1000 PX** document. Press **D** to switch to the default background and foreground colors. Choose **Render | Fibers** from the **Filter** menu. In the **Fibers** dialog box that appears, set the values as shown in Fig. T2 and click **OK**.

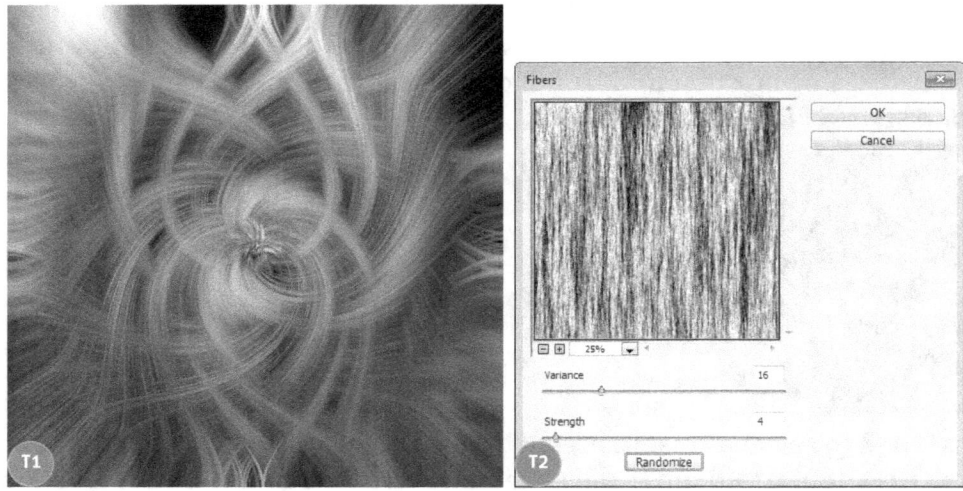

Creating the Design

Follow the steps given next:

1. Choose **Filter Gallery | Sketch | Plaster** from the **Filter** menu. Set the values as shown in Fig. T3 and then click **OK**. Choose **Filter Gallery | Brush Strokes | Sprayed Strokes** from the **Filter** menu.

2. Set the values as shown in Fig. T4 and then click **OK**. Choose **Blur | Radial Blur** from the **Filter** menu. In the **Radial Blur** dialog box that opens, set the values as shown in Fig. T5, and then click **OK**. Fig. T6 shows the result.

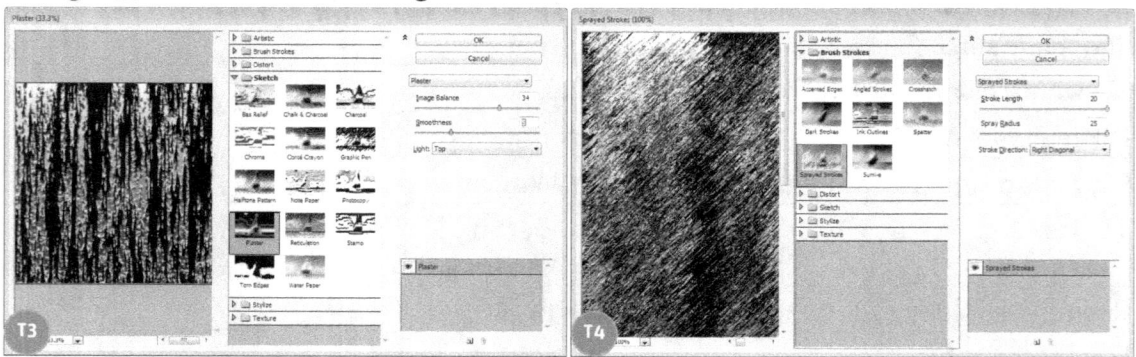

Chapter F4 - Creating Background Designs

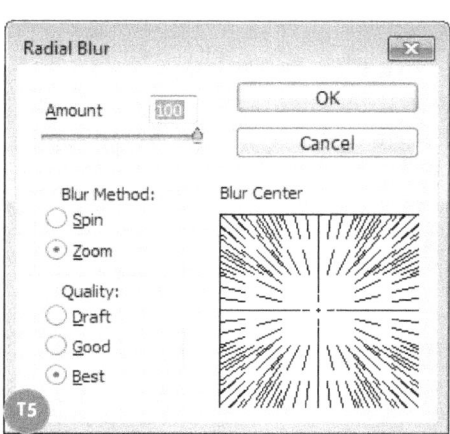
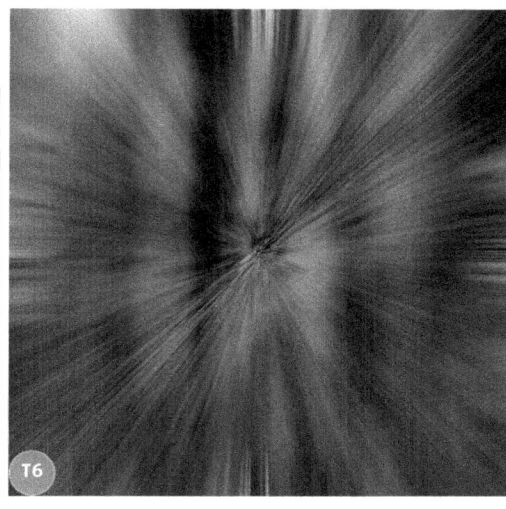

3. Make two copies of the **Background** layer and rename them as **Layer 1** and **Layer 2**. Select **Layer 1** and then choose **Distort | Twirl** from the **Filter** menu. In the **Twirl** dialog box that appears, set **Angle** to **158** and then clock **OK**. Select **Layer 2** and then choose **Distort | Twirl** from the **Filter** menu. In the **Twirl** dialog box that appears, set **Angle** to **-158** and then clock **OK**.

4. Select **Layer 2** and set its **Blending Mode** to **Lighten**. Similarly, set **Layer 1**'s **Blending Mode** to **Lighten**. Press **Ctrl+U**. In the **Hue/Saturation** dialog box that appears, set the values as shown in Fig. T7 and then click **OK**. Select **Layer 1** and set its **Blending Mode** to **Lighten**. Press **Ctrl+U**. In the **Hue/Saturation** dialog box that appears, set the values as shown in Fig. T8 and then click **OK**. Select **Layer 1** and press **Alt+Shift+Ctrl+L**. Repeat the process for **Layer 2**.

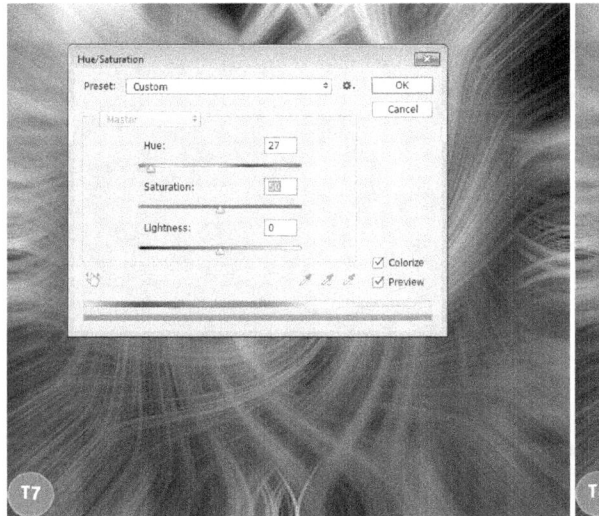
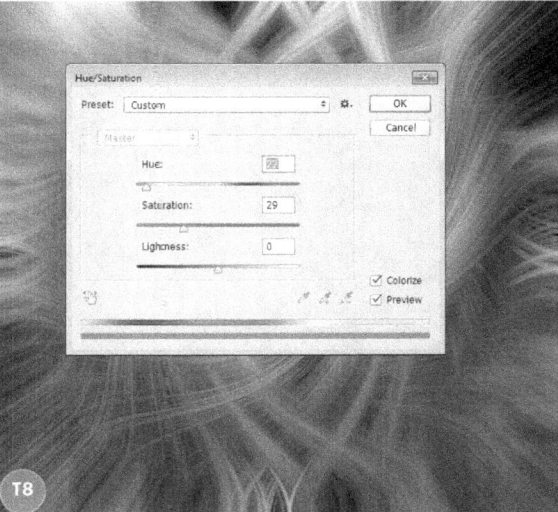

Summary
In this chapter:

- 10 Tutorials covering background design creation techniques
- Covers the following filters: **Difference Clouds, Patchwork, Motion Blur, Trace Contour, Halftone Pattern, Lens Flare, Wave, Chrome, Plaster, Twirl, Fibers, Water Paper, Emboss, Clouds, Radial Blur, Sprayed Strokes,** and **Sketch**

IN THIS CHAPTER:

- 10 tutorials covering texture creation techniques.
- Covers the following filters: **Difference Clouds, High Pass, Add Noise, Gaussian Blur, Wind, Texturizer, Halftone Pattern, Sumi-e, Water Paper, Stained Glass, Motion Blur, Emboss, Paint Daubs, Offset,** and **Plastic Wrap**

Chapter F5

Creating Textures

In this chapter, we will create textures using filters. You can use these textures in your design project or you can use them to texture the 3D models. This chapter also covers the techniques to create maps such as bump, refection, diffuse, and so on for your 3D models.

Photoshop CC 2017

Tutorials

Before you start the tutorials, create a folder with the name **chapter-f5**. We'll use this folder to host all the tutorial files and other resources.

Tutorial 1: Creating Marble Texture

Let's start with creating a marble texture [Fig. T1] using filters and image adjustment commands. In the process, we will learn about equalizing images in Photoshop. Before tiling your textures, you need to fix problems such as uneven brightness, visible seams, and shift in colors.

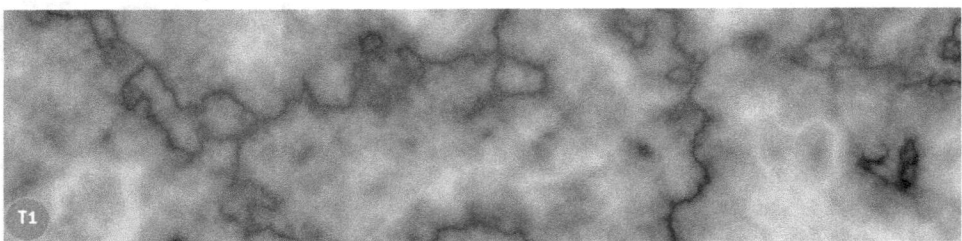

The following table summarizes the tutorial:

Table T1	
Flow: *The following sequence will be used in this tutorial:* *1. Create a new Photoshop document. 2. Use the **Difference Clouds** filter to create the marble texture. 3. Use the **High Pass** filter to sharp the colors. 4. Use the **Shadows/Highlight, Exposure**, and **Color Balance** commands to color correct the texture.*	
Keywords: *Difference Clouds, High Pass, Color Balance, Exposure, and Shadows/Highlights*	
Difficulty level	Intermediate
Estimated time to complete	15 Minutes
Resources folder	**chapter-f5**
Final tutorial file	**f5_tut1_finish.psd**

Follow the steps given next:

1. Open **Photoshop** and create a **1000x1000** px document. Unlock the **Background** layer and then press **D** to set the black and white colors for the foreground and background, respectively. Choose **Render | Difference Clouds** from the **Filter** menu to apply the filter on the **Layer 0** layer [Fig. T2].

> **Note: Difference Clouds Filter**
> The **Difference Clouds** filter randomly generates values between the foreground and background colors to create a cloud pattern. This filter blends the colors in the same way the **Difference** mode blends. The first time you apply this filter, a cloud pattern is created by Photoshop. If you apply this filter repeatedly, ribs and veins are created that resembles a marble texture.

2. Repeatedly apply the **Difference Clouds** filter until you get the basic marble texture you are looking for [Fig. T3]. Duplicate **Layer 0** and rename it as **Layer 1**. Choose **Blur | Average** from the **Filter** menu to apply filter to **Layer 1** [Fig. T4]. The **Average** filter averages color of an image or selection and then fill the image or selection with that color. It helps in creating smooth looking textures.

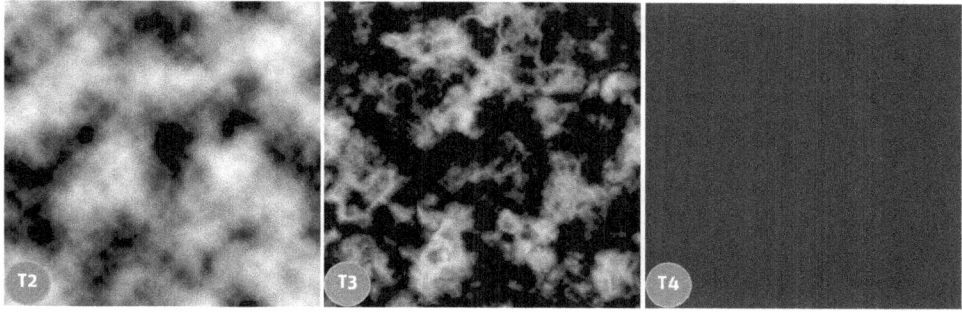

> **Warning: Transparent Pixels**
> Unexpected results are produced if you average pixels from the transparent regions.

3. Place **Layer 1** underneath **Layer 0** in the **Layers** panel. Set the **Blending Mode** of **Layer 0** to **Linear Light** and then set **Opacity** to **50%**. Make sure **Layer 0** is selected and then choose **Other | High Pass** from the **Filter** menu. In the **High Pass** dialog box that appears, set **Radius** to **120** and click **OK** [refer to Fig. T5].

> **Note: High Pass Filter**
> The **High Pass** filter allows you to retain the edge details in the specified radius where sharp color transitions occur in the image. It then suppresses the rest of the image. This filter creates a smooth version of the image. For tutorial, if you apply this filter to a grass texture, it will convert the image to a homogeneous patch of green [see the image on the right].

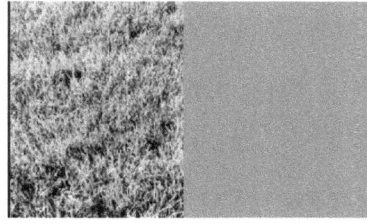

> **Note: High Pass Filter**
> This filter produces the opposite effect that of the **Gaussian Blur** filter.

> **Tip: Extracting Line Art**
> This filter is useful in extracting line art and large black and white areas from the scanned images.

4. Choose **Adjustments | Shadows/Highlights** from the **Image** menu. In the **Shadows/Highlights** dialog box that appears, set **Amount** to **100** in the **Shadows** group. Make sure **Amount** in the **Highlights** group is set to **0** and then click **OK** [Fig. T6].

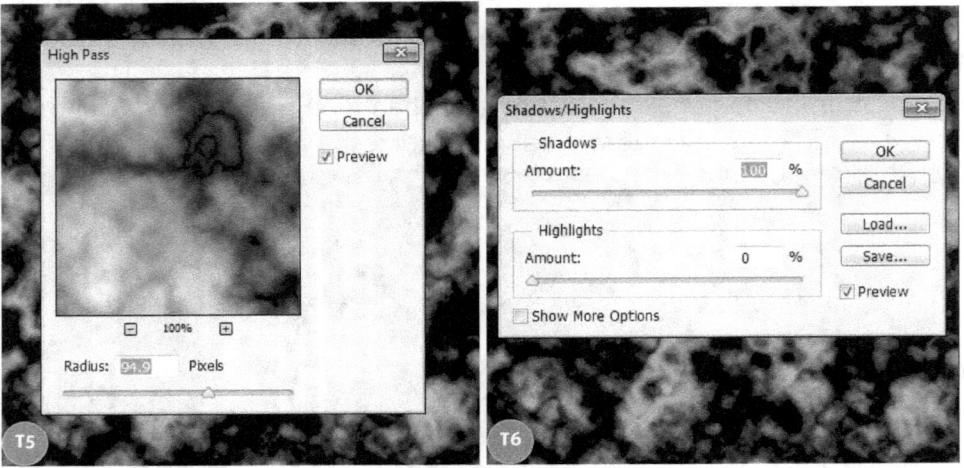

The **Shadows/Highlights** command lightens or darkens the image based on the surrounding pixels. The default values in the **Shadows/Highlights** dialog box are meant for fixing images having backlight problem.

> **Note: Shadows/Highlights Command**
> You can also use this command to correct washed out images because they were close to the camera flash.

5. Choose **Adjustments | Color Balance** from the **Image** menu. In the **Color Balance** dialog box that appears, set the values as shown in Fig. T7 and then click **OK**.

The **Color Balance** command allows you to change the overall mix of the colors in the image. You can use this command for a generalized color correction.

6. Press **Ctrl+E** to merge the layers. Choose **Adjustments | Exposure** from the **Image** menu. In the **Exposure** dialog box that appears, set **Exposure** to **0.65** and **Offset** to **-0.0244**. Press **Ctrl+S** to save the document.

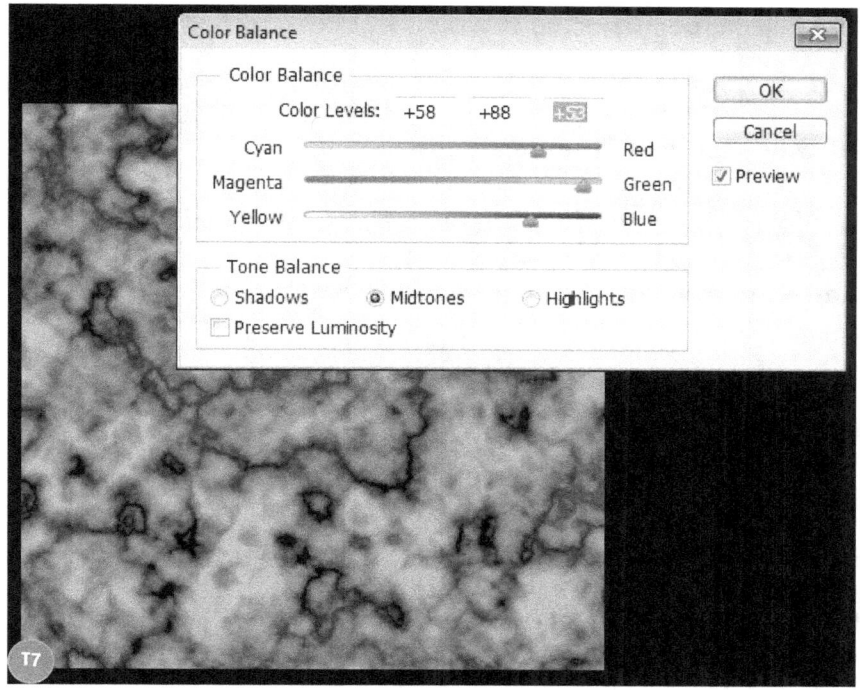

○ *Tip: Equalize Command*
You can also use the **Equalize** command from the **Image | Adjustments** menu. The **Equalize** command redistributes the brightness values so that they represent entire range of the brightness values.

○ *Tip: Hue/Saturation command*
Use the **Hue/Saturation** command if you want to change the color of the marble.

Note: Exposure Command
The **Exposure** command is primarily used with HDR images. It adjusts tonality of the image in the **Linear** color space.

Tutorial 2: Creating Door Mat Texture

In this tutorial, we will create a door mat texture [Fig. T1]. You can use the same technique to create various types of fabrics and special effects.

Photoshop CC 2017

The following table summarizes the tutorial:

Table T2	
Flow: *The following sequence will be used in this tutorial:* *1. Create a new Photoshop document. 2. Use the **Add Noise**, **Gaussian Blur**, and **Wind** filters to create texture.*	
Keywords: *Add Noise, Gaussian Blur, Wind, and Horizontal Type*	
Difficulty level	Beginner
Estimated time to complete	15 Minutes
Resources folder	**chapter-f5**
Final tutorial file	**f5_tut2_finish.psd**

Follow the steps given next:

1. Open **Photoshop** and create a **960x540px** document. Fill the document with **50%** gray using the **Edit | Fill** command. Choose **Noise | Add Noise** from the **Filter** menu and then set the parameters, as shown in Fig. T2. Click **OK**.

 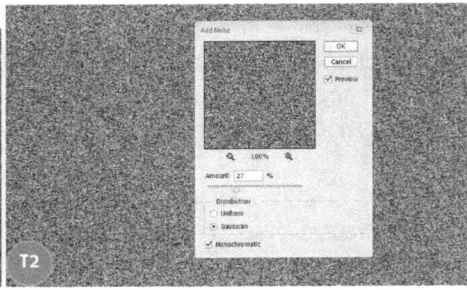

> *Note: Add Noise Filter*
>
> *The **Add Noise** filter applies random pixels to an image. You can use this filter in a variety of ways, from reducing banding from the feathered selections to give realistic looks to the heavily retouched areas, from making a texture realistic to creating special effects.*
>
> *It provides two options for noise distribution: **Uniform** and **Gaussian**. The **Uniform** method creates a subtle effect whereas the **Gaussian** method produces a speckled effect. You can use the **Monochromatic** option if you just want to affect the tonal values leaving the color unchanged.*

2. Choose **Blur | Gaussian Blur** from the **Filter** menu and then set **Radius** to **1** in the **Gaussian Blur** dialog box that appears. Click **OK**. Choose **Stylize | Wind** from the **Filter** menu and then select **Stagger** from the **Method** section. Select **From the Left** from the **Direction** section [Fig. T3]. Click **OK**.

> *Note: Wind Filter*
> The **Wind** filter applies tiny lines to the image simulating a windblown effect. It has three types: **Wind**, **Blast**, and **Stagger**. The **Stagger** is more dramatic than the other two methods. This method offsets lines in the image [see the images below] for the three methods, respectively.

3. Unlock the **Background** layer and apply the **Color Overlay** style to it [Fig. T4]. Use the following color: **#964605**.

4. Pick **Crop Tool** from **Tool Box** and then RMB click on the canvas, choose **1x1 [Square]** from the popup menu that appears. Press **Enter** to commit the changes [Fig. T5]. Now, if you check the size of the image, it should be **540x540px**. Notice in Fig. T5, the fiber strands are not oriented correctly. We need to change their orientation to vertical. Let's do it.

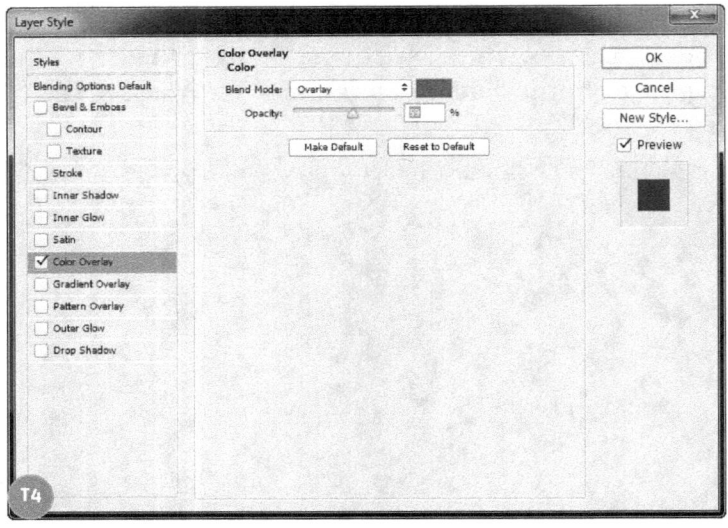

> **Note: High-res Seamless Texture**
> Use the technique explained in Tutorial 1 to create a high-res seamless texture.

5. Choose **Image Rotation | 90 Counter Clockwise** from the **Image** menu to change the orientation of the strands [Fig. T6]. Now, let's add some text [**Welcome**] on the texture and apply some styling to it. Pick **Horizontal Type Tool** from **Tool Box** and type "**Welcome**" using a font of your choice. Set **Fill** to **0%** for the **Welcome** layer. Apply the **Inner Shadow** layer style to the **Welcome** layer [Fig. T7]. Now, apply the **Stroke** layer style [Fig. T8]. Press **Ctrl+S** to save the file. Fig. T1 shows the end result.

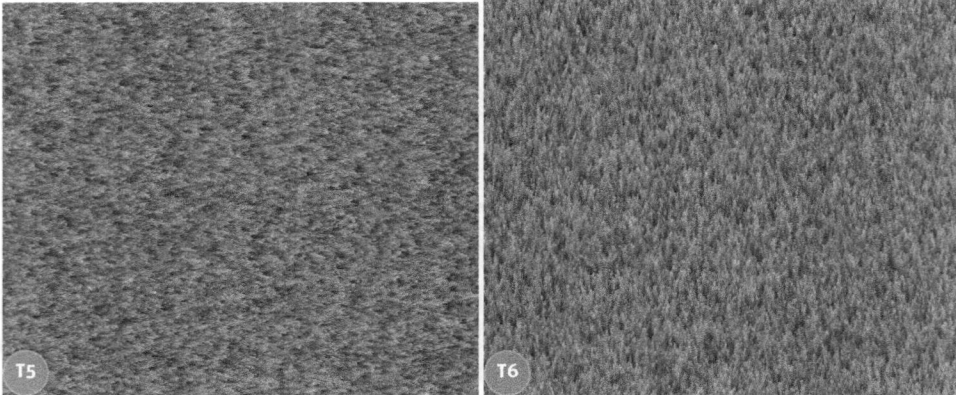

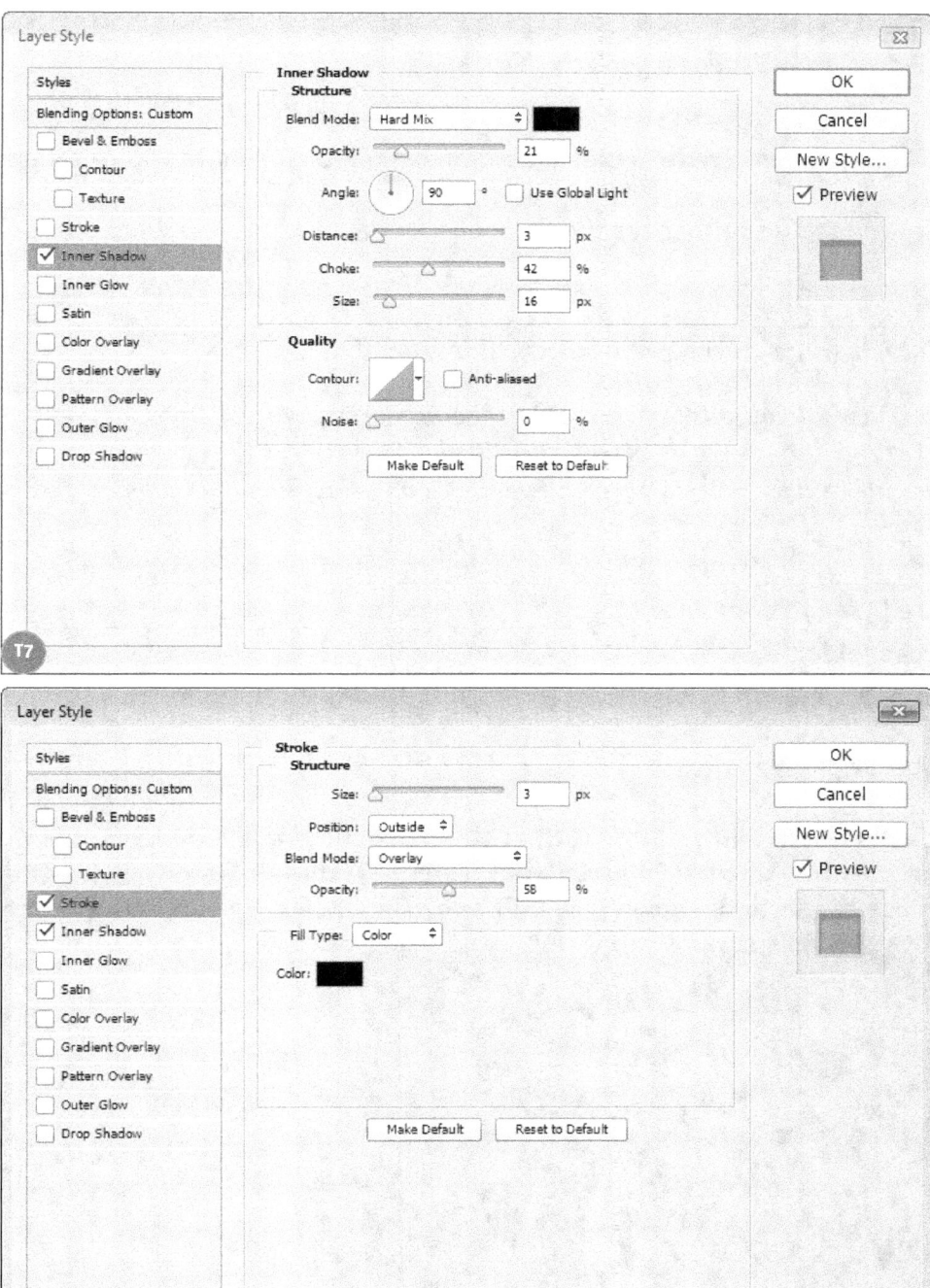

Tip: Wide Fonts
Wider fonts will appear good on this texture.

Tutorial 3: Creating Military Camouflage Texture

In this tutorial, we will create a green camouflage texture using various filters [Fig. T1].

The following table summarizes the tutorial:

Table T3	
Flow: The following sequence will be used in this tutorial:	
1. Create a new Photoshop document. 2. Use the **Texturizer, Water Paper, Difference Clouds, Gaussian Blur, Sumi-e,** and **Halftone Pattern** filters to create texture.	
Keywords: Texturizer, Water Paper, Difference Clouds, Gaussian Blur, Sumi-e, and Halftone Pattern	
Difficulty level	Beginner
Estimated time to complete	20 Minutes
Resources folder	**chapter-f5**
Final tutorial file	**f5_tut3_finish.psd**

Follow the steps given next:

1. Open **Photoshop** and create a **1000x1000** px document. Fill the document with the color: **#394f25**. Choose **Filter Gallery | Texture | Texturizer** from the **Filter** menu and then use the settings shown in Fig. T2 and click **OK**. Fig. T3 shows the texture.

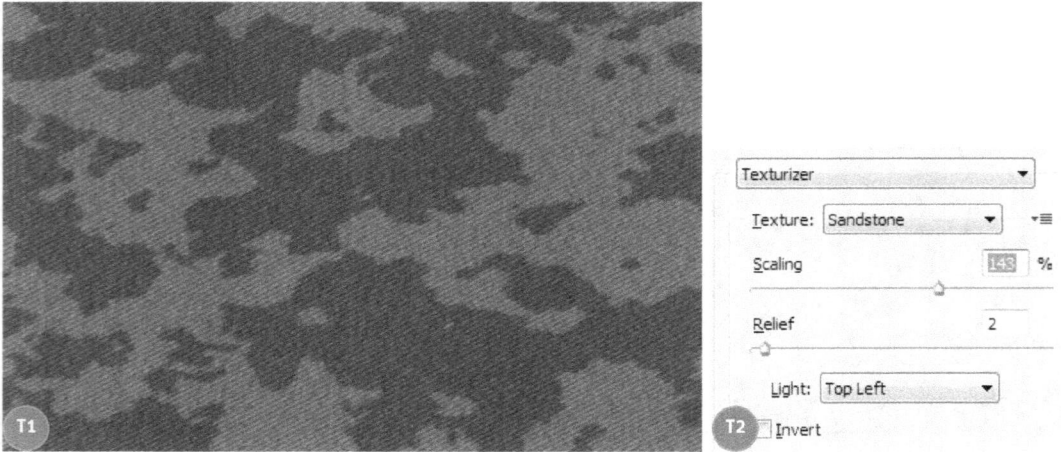

> **Note: Texturizer Filter**
> The **Texturizer** filter applies a texture to the image. It has four built-in textures: **Brick, Burlap, Canvas,** and **Sandstone** [see the images below].

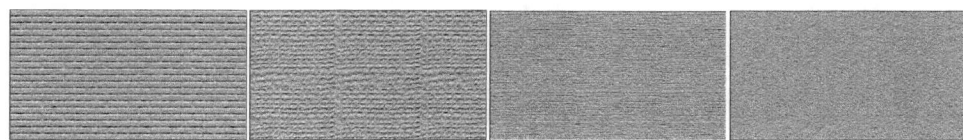

You can also load your custom texture by using the drop-down located next to the **Texture** parameter [refer Fig. T2]. The **Light** parameter can be used to change the direction of the light. Fig. on the right shows the **Brick** texture with **Light** set to **Bottom Right**.

2. Unlock the **Background** layer and then create a copy of it. Rename the new layer as **Layer 1**. Choose **Filter Gallery | Sketch | Water Paper** from the **Filter** menu and then use the settings shown in Fig. T4. Set the **Blending Mode** to **Linear Light** and **Opacity** to **24%**. Fig. T5 shows the texture.

> **Note: Water Paper Filter**
> The **Water Paper** filter produces blotchy daub that appears to be carelessly painted on a damp paper.

3. Duplicate **Layer 0** and rename it as **Layer 2**. Move it to the top of the stack. Choose **Filter Gallery | Sketch | Halftone Pattern** from the **Filter** menu and then use the settings shown in Fig. T6. Click **OK**.

Note: Halftone Pattern
The **Halftone** Pattern simulates the effect of a halftone screen. This filter maintains the continuous range of tones. This filter can produce three patterns: **Circle**, **Dot**, and **Line** [see images below].

4. Select **Layer 0** and **Layer 1** an then press **Ctrl+E** to merge them. Duplicate **Layer 2** and rename it **Layer 3**. Make sure **Layer 3** is selected and then press **Ctrl+T** to transform. Rotate the layer as shown in Fig. T7. Also, scale the image so that it covers whole canvas.

5. Press **Enter** to apply the transform. Ensure **Layer 3** is selected in the **Layers** panel and then choose **Blur | Gaussian Blur** from the **Filter** menu. In the **Gaussian Blur** dialog box that appears, set **Radius** to **1.6** and then click **OK** [Fig. T8].

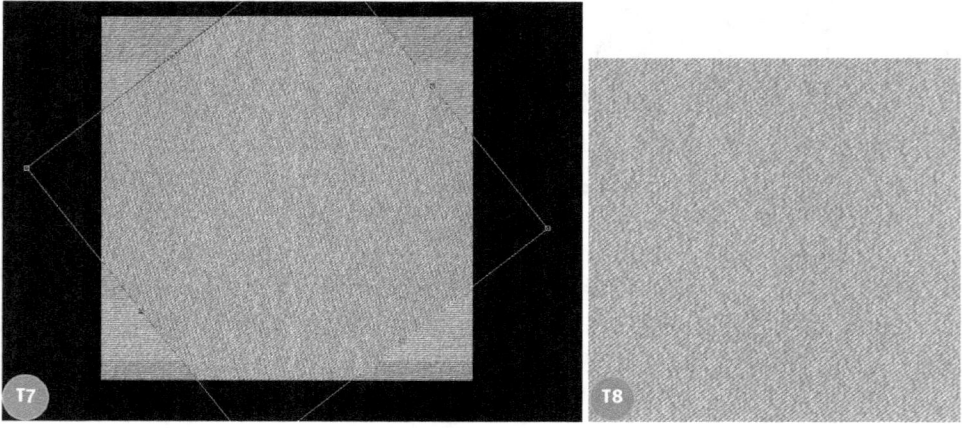

> **Note: Gaussian Blur Filter**
> The **Gaussian Blur** filter blurs [add low frequency details] an image by an adjustable amount. The term **Gaussian** refers to the bell-shaped curve that Photoshop generates when it applies a weighted average to the pixels.

6. Set the **Blending Mode** for **Layer 3** to **Linear Light** and **Opacity** to **24%**. Set the **Blending Mode** for **Layer 2** to **Soft Light** [Fig. T9]. Choose **Flatten Image** from the **Layer** menu. Create new layer and rename it as **Layer 4**, fill it with **50%** Gray using the **Edit | Fill** command. Press **D**.

7. Choose **Render | Difference Clouds** from the **Filter** menu. Choose **Adjustments | Equalize** from the **Image** menu [Fig. T10]. Choose **Adjustments | Threshold** from the **Image** menu. In the **Threshold** dialog box that appears, set **Threshold Level** to **131** and then click **OK** [Fig. T11].

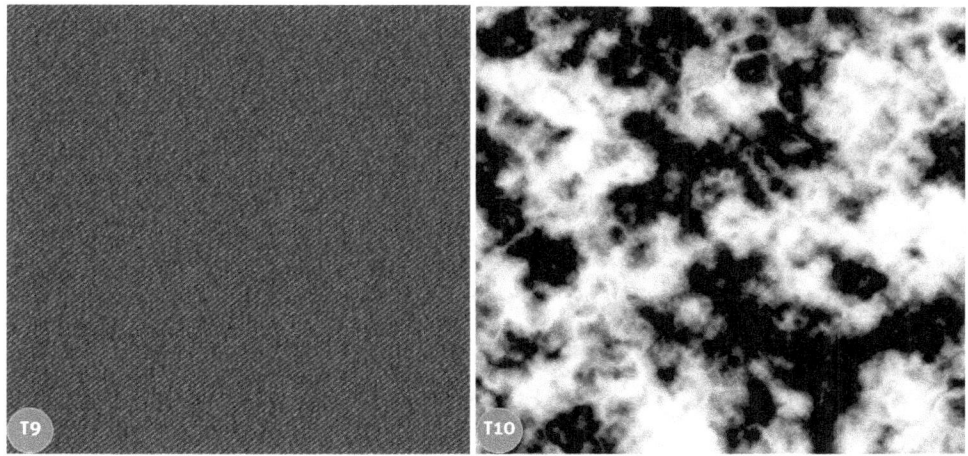

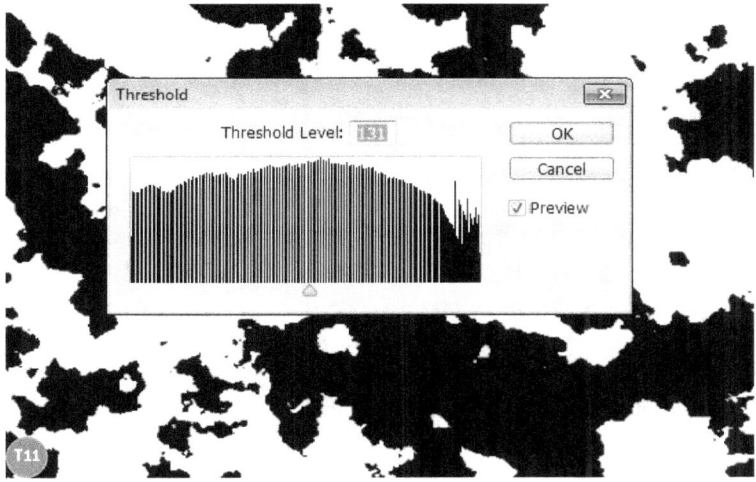

> **Note: Threshold Filter**
> The **Threshold** command converts the images to high-contrast, black-and-white images. All pixels lighter than the threshold value are converted to white whereas all pixels darker are converted to black.

8. Set **Blending Mode** to **Overlay** for **Layer 4** and then set **Opacity** to **18%**. Choose **Filter Gallery | Brush Strokes | Sumi-e** from the **Filter** menu and then use the settings shown in Fig. T12. Click **OK**. Fig. T1 shows the final result.

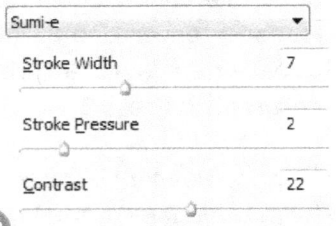

T12

> **Note: Sumi-e Filter**
> **Sumi-e** is a Japanese style filter. It produces effects like a fully saturated brush applied to a rice paper. This filter creates soft blurred edges with rich black.

Tutorial 4: Creating Leather Texture

In this tutorial, we will create a leather texture, Fig. T1.

The following table summarizes the tutorial:

Table T4	
Flow: The following sequence will be used in this tutorial: 1. Create a new Photoshop document. 2. Use the **Stained Glass** and **Texturizer** filters to create texture.	
Keywords: Stained Glass and Texturizer	
Difficulty level	Intermediate
Estimated time to complete	20 Minutes
Resources folder	**chapter-f5**
Final tutorial file	**f5_tut4_finish.psd**

1. Create a new **1000x1000 px** Photoshop document with the default background and foreground colors. Choose **Filter Gallery | Texture | Stained Glass** from the **Filter** menu and then set **Cell Size** to **5**, **Border Thickness** to **4**, and **Light Intensity** to **2** [Fig. T2]. Click **OK**.

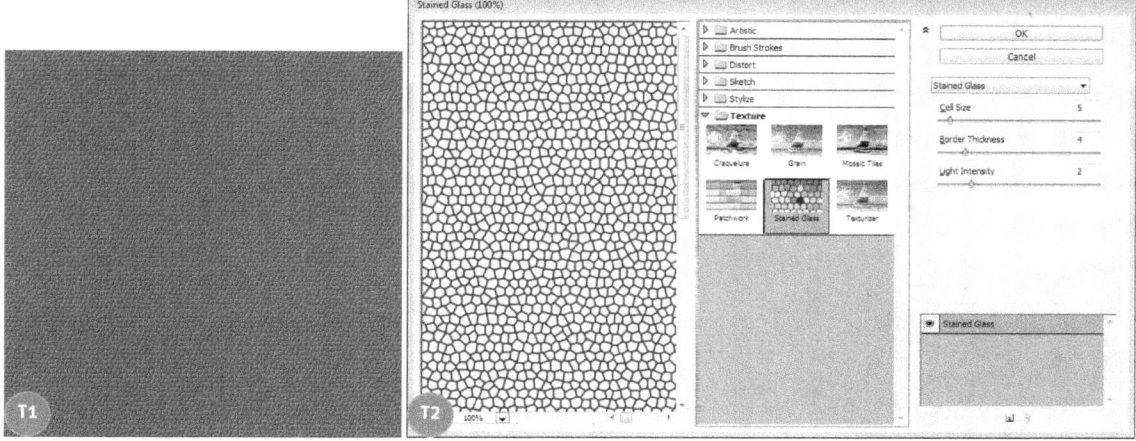

2. Save the document with the name **displaceMap.psd**. Create a new **1000x1000** px Photoshop document and fill it with the **#9D7a51** color. Choose **Filter Gallery | Texture | Texturizer** from the **Filter** menu and then set **Texture** to **Sandstone**, **Scaling** to **60**, and **Relief** to **2**. Select **Light** to **Top** [Fig. T3] and then click **OK**.

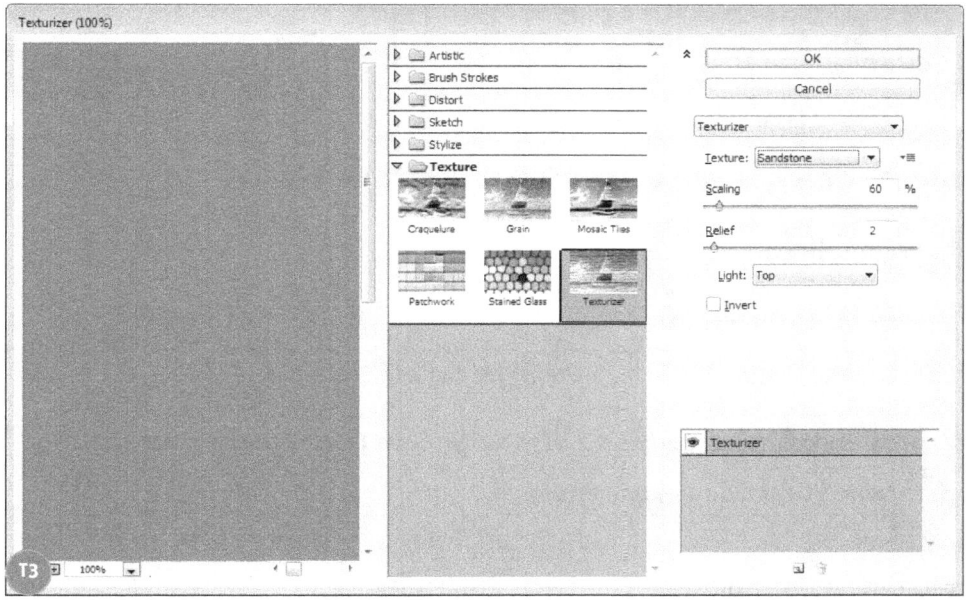

3. Choose **Filter Gallery | Texture | Texturizer** from the **Filter** menu and then select **Load Texture** from the **Texture** options [Fig. T4]. In the **Load Texture** dialog box that appears, select **displaceMap.psd** and then click **Open**. Set **Scaling** to **100**, **Relief** to **4**, and **Light** to **Top Left** [Fig. T5]. Click **OK**. Press **Ctrl+L** and then adjust the levels [Fig. T6]. Save the document.

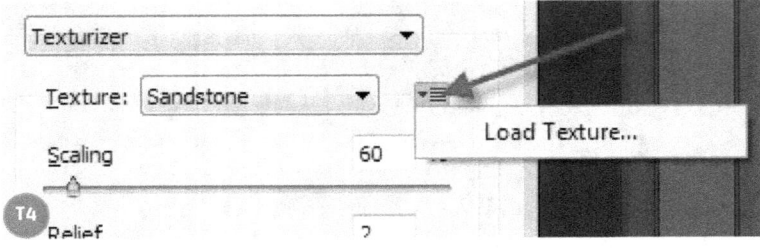

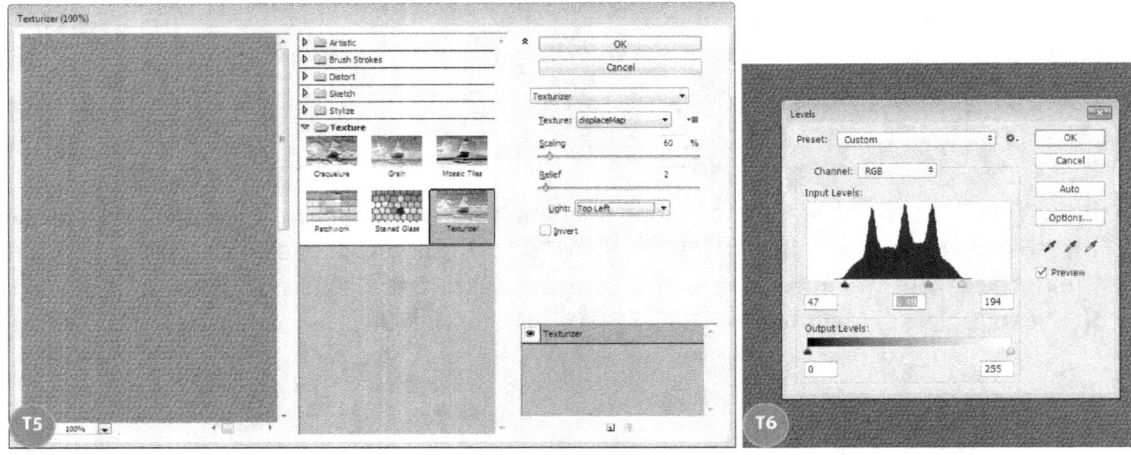

Tutorial 5: Creating Lattice Wire Mesh Texture

In this tutorial, we will create lattice wire mesh texture, Fig. T1.

The following table summarizes the tutorial:

Table T5	
Flow: *The following sequence will be used in this tutorial:*	
1. Create a new Photoshop document. 2. Use the Stained Glass filter to create texture.	
Keywords: *Stained Glass, and Magic Wand*	
Difficulty level	Beginner
Estimated time to complete	15 Minutes
Resources folder	**chapter-f5**
Final tutorial file	**f5_tut5_finish.psd**

Follow the steps given next:

1. Create a new **1000x1000** px Photoshop document with the default background and foreground colors. Unlock the **Background** layer. Choose **Filter Gallery | Texture | Stained Glass** from the **Filter** menu and then set **Cell Size** to 10, **Border Thickness** to 4, and **Light Intensity** to 3 [Fig. T2]. Click **OK**.

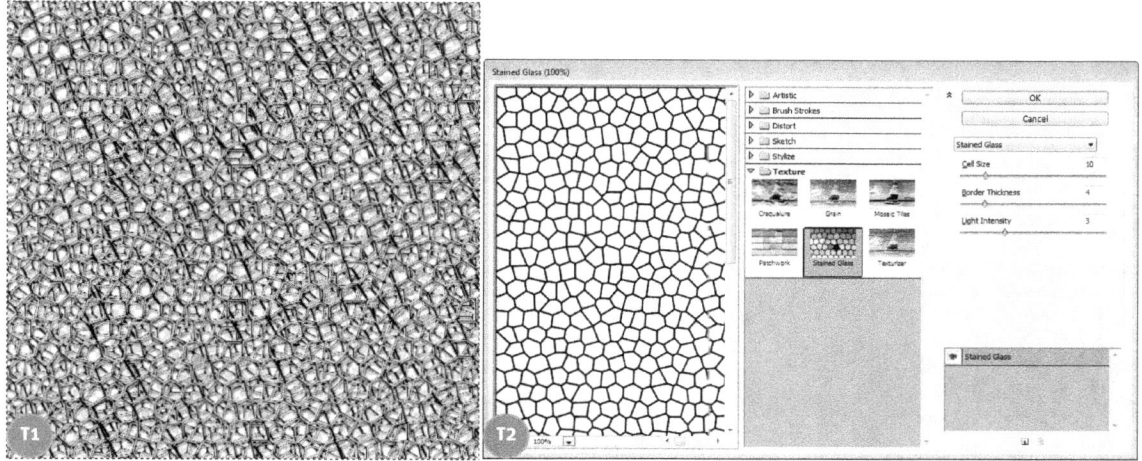

> **Note: Stained Glass Filter**
> This filter repaints the image as single colored adjacent cells. The cells are outlined in the foreground color.

2. Pick **Magic Wand Tool** from **Tool Box** and then click on the black area of the layer. Press **Ctrl+Shift+I** to invert the selection and press **Delete** to remove the pixels [Fig. T3]. Press **Ctrl+D** to clear the selection. Apply the **Bevel & Emboss** layer style to the **Layer 0** and then set the values as shown in Fig. T4.

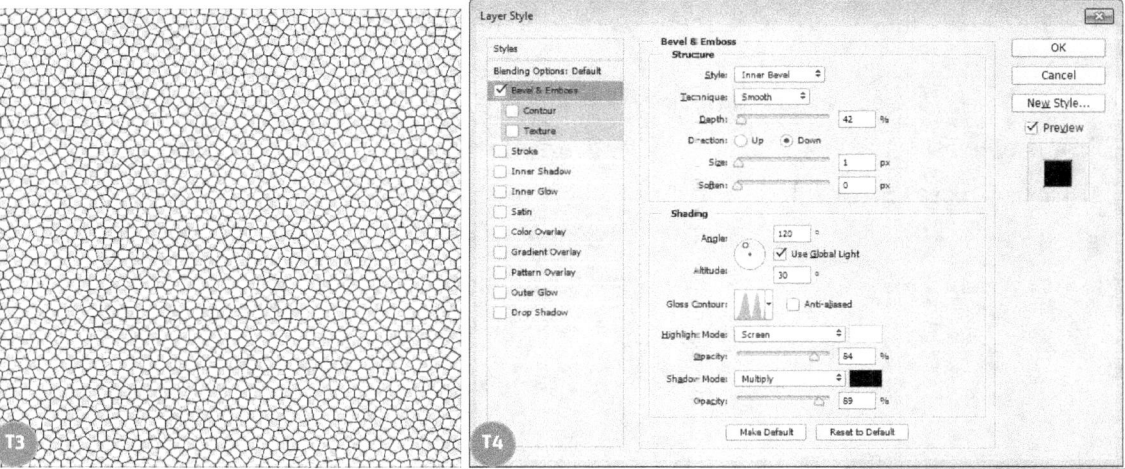

3. Now, apply **Inner Glow** style, refer Fig. T5. Add the **Drop Shadow** style with **Size** and **Distance** set to **2**. Duplicate **Layer 0** and then flip the duplicate layer by choosing **Transform | Flip Horizontal** from the **Edit** menu. Create another copy of the layer and change its position slightly using arrow keys [Fig. T6].

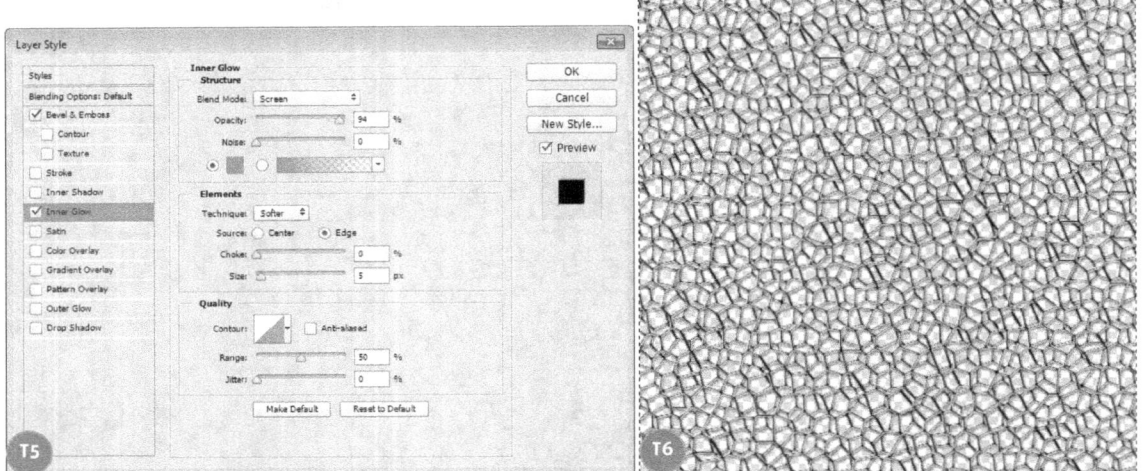

4. Remove the unwanted portion of the image using the **Crop Tool**.

Tutorial 6: Creating Brushed Metal Texture

In this tutorial, we will create brushed metal texture, Fig. T1.

The following table summarizes the tutorial:

Table T6	
Flow: *The following sequence will be used in this tutorial:* *1. Create a new Photoshop document. 2. Use the **Texturizer**, **Motion Blur**, and **Add Noise** filters to create texture.*	
Keywords: *Texturizer, Motion Blur, and Add Noise*	
Difficulty level	Intermediate
Estimated time to complete	15 Minutes
Resources folder	**chapter-f5**
Final tutorial file	**f5_tut6_finish.psd**

Follow the steps given next:

1. Create a new **1000x1000 px** Photoshop document with the **50%** gray background. Choose **Noise | Add Noise** from the **Filter** menu to open the **Add Noise** dialog box.

2. In this dialog box, set **Amount** to **10**, **Distribution** to **Gaussian**, and the click **OK** [Fig. T2].

3. Choose **Blur | Motion Blur** from the **Filter** menu. In the **Motion Blur** dialog box that opens, set **Angle** to **0**, **Distance** to **2000**, and then click **OK** [Fig. T3].

4. Save the document with the name **metalDisplace.psd**. Create a new **1000x1000** px Photoshop document with the **50%** gray background. Choose **Noise | Add Noise** from the **Filter** menu to open the **Add Noise** dialog box. In this dialog box, set **Amount** to **2**, **Distribution** to **Gaussian**, and the click **OK**.

5. Choose **Filter Gallery | Texture | Texturizer** from the **Filter** menu and then select **Load Texture** from the **Texture** options. In the **Load Texture** dialog box that appears, select **metalDisplace.psd** and then click **Open**.

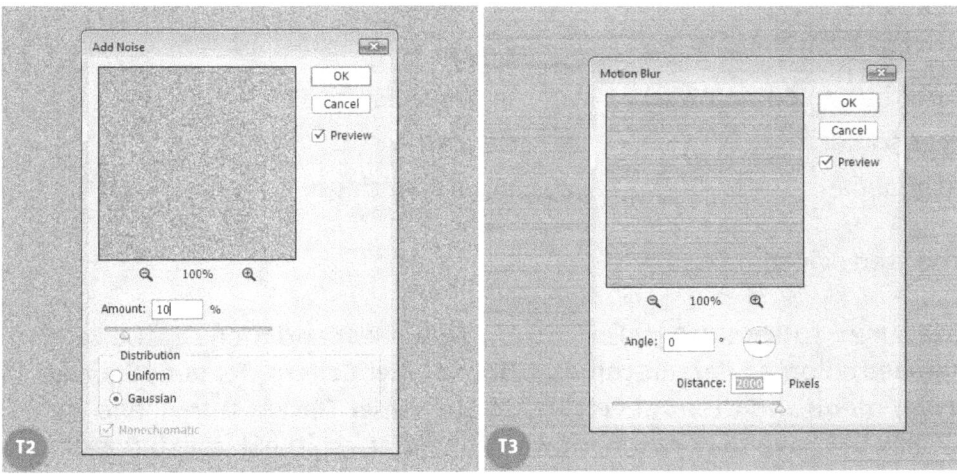

6. Set **Scaling** to **100**, **Relief** to **13**, and **Light** to **Top Left** [Fig. T4]. Click **OK**. Unlock the **Background** layer and apply **Gradient Overlay** style on it, refer Fig. T5 for values.

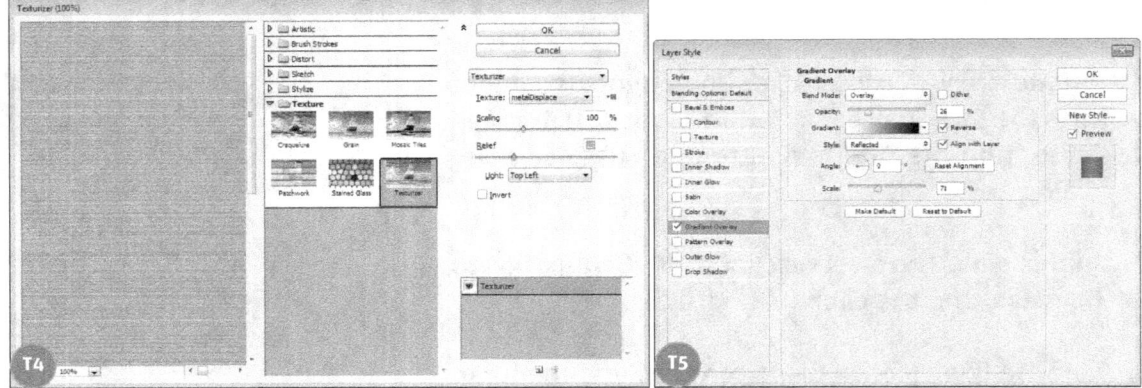

Tutorial 7: Creating Reptile Skin Texture

In this tutorial, we will create reptile skin texture, refer Fig. T1.

The following table summarizes the tutorial:

Table T7	
Flow: *The following sequence will be used in this tutorial:* *1. Create a new Photoshop document. 2. Use the **Stained Glass** and **Texturizer** filters to create texture.*	
Keywords: *Stained Glass, Texturizer, and Magic Wand*	
Difficulty level	Beginner
Estimated time to complete	15 Minutes
Resources folder	**chapter-f5**
Final tutorial file	**f5_tut7_finish.psd**

Follow the steps given next:

1. Create a new **1000x1000** px Photoshop document and then set the **Foreground** and **Background** colors to default values. Choose **Filter Gallery | Texture | Stained Glass** from the **Filter** menu and then set **Cell Size** to **10**, **Border Thickness** to **4**, and **Light Intensity** to **3**. Click **OK**. Save the document with the name **repltileSkinTexture.psd**.

2. Create a new **1000x1000** px Photoshop document and then fill the background with the **#86441a**.

3. Ensure **repltileSkinTexture.psd** is open and then select the black color using **Magic Wand Tool**. Press **Ctrl+C** to copy the pixels. Now, press **Ctrl+V** to paste the pixels in the document created in Step 2 [Fig. T2].

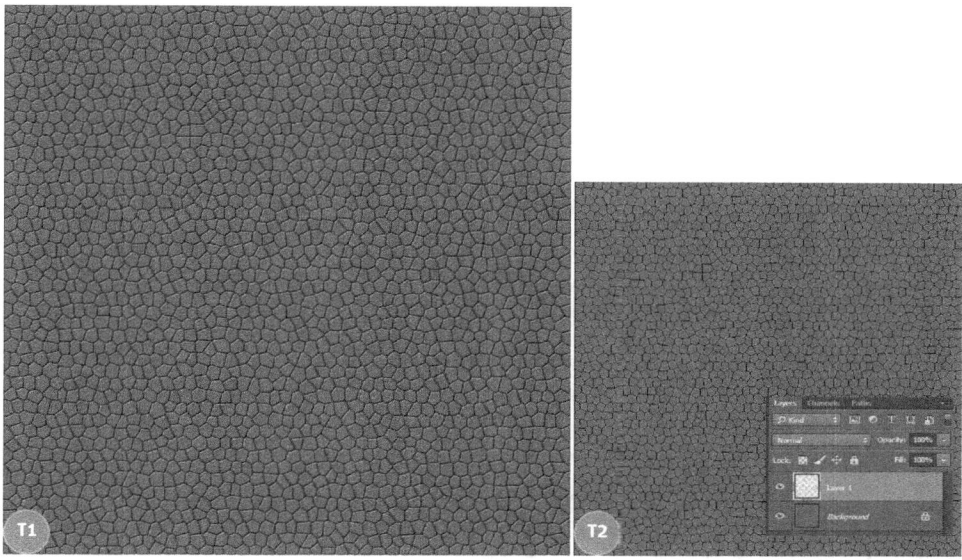

4. Ensure the **Background** layer is selected and then choose **Filter Gallery | Texture | Texturizer** from the **Filter** menu. Then, select **Load Texture** from the **Texture** options. In the **Load Texture** dialog box that appears, select the **reptileSkinTexture.psd** as **Texture**.

5. Also, set **Scaling** to **100**, and **Relief** to **3**. Select **Light** to **Top Left** [Fig. T3] and then click **OK**. Select **Layer 1** and apply the **Color Overlay** style to it. Use the **#542103** color. Fig. T4 shows the result. Apply **Bevel & Emboss**, and **Drop Shadow** layer styles [refer Figs. T5 and T6 for settings]. Fig. T7 shows the result.

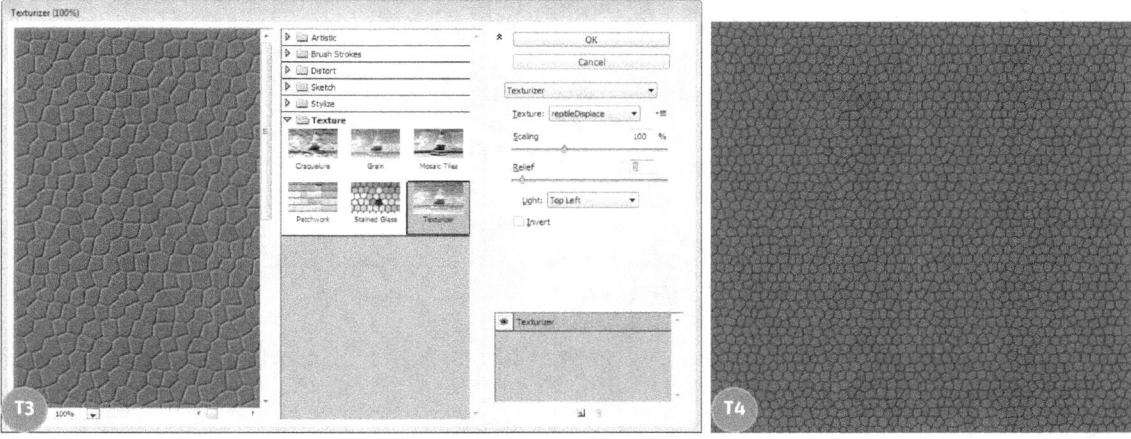

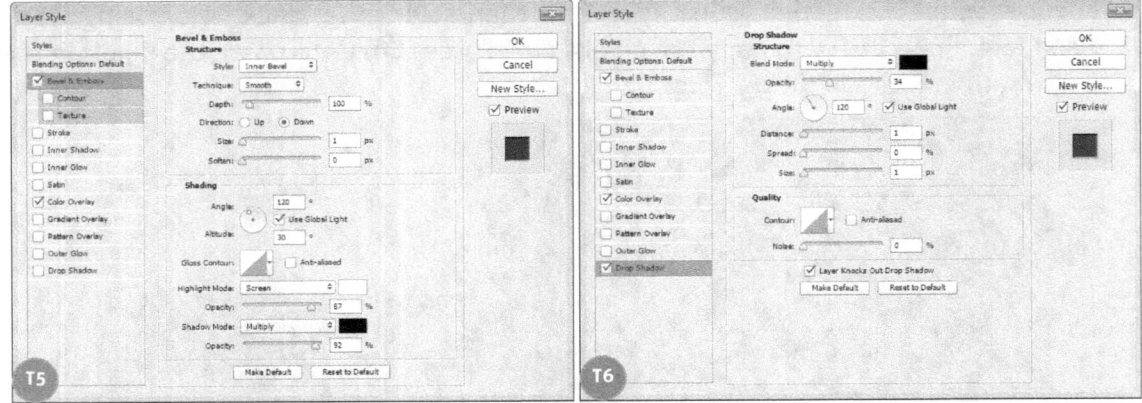

6. Press **Ctrl+A** followed by **Ctrl+Shift+C** to copy the merged pixels and then press **Ctrl+V** to paste them. Choose **Filter Gallery | Texture | Texturizer** from the **Filter** menu and then set **Texture** to **Sandstone**, **Scaling** to **100**, and **Relief** to **2**. Select **Light** to **Top** [Fig. T8] and then click **OK**.

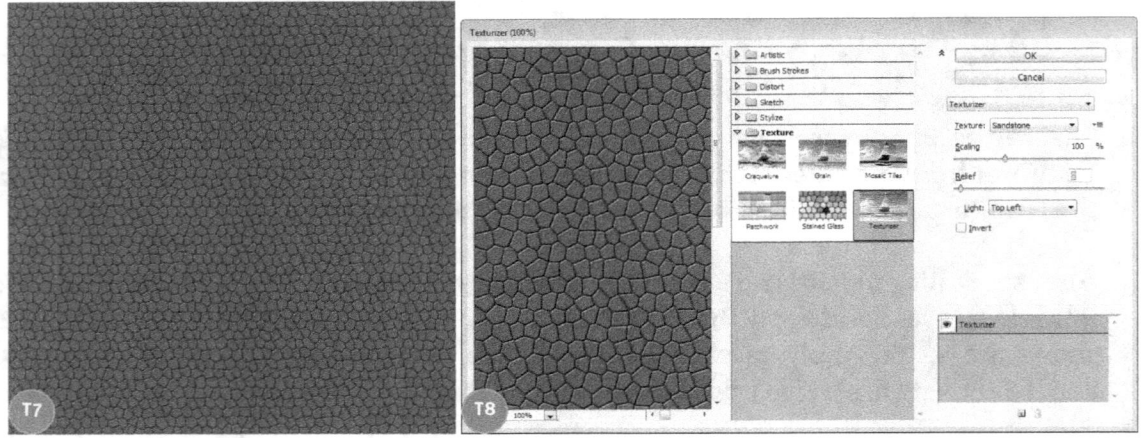

Tutorial 8 : Creating Sand Texture

In this tutorial, we will create the sand texture, Fig. T1.

The following table summarizes the tutorial:

Table T8
Flow: *The following sequence will be used in this tutorial:*
*1. Create a new Photoshop document. 2. Use the **Clouds**, **Add Noise**, and **Texturizer** filters to create texture.*
Keywords: *Clouds, Add Noise, and Texturizer*

Table T8	
Difficulty level	Intermediate
Estimated time to complete	30 Minutes
Resources folder	**chapter-f5**
Final tutorial file	**f5_tut8_finish.psd**

Follow the steps given next:

1. Create a new **1000x1000** px Photoshop document and then set the **Foreground** and **Background** colors to default values. Choose **Render | Clouds** from the **Filter** menu.

    Note: Clouds Filter
   *The **Clouds** filter allows you to create a cloud pattern using the values that transition between the foreground and background colors.*

    Tip: Dark cloud pattern
   *If you want to create a dark cloud pattern, hold **Alt** and then choose **Render | Clouds** from the **Filter** menu.*

    Caution: Clouds Filter
   *When you apply the **Clouds** filter, the pixels on the active layer are replaced by the cloud pattern.*

2. Choose **Noise | Add Noise** from the **Filter** menu to open the **Add Noise** dialog box. In this dialog box, set **Amount** to **5**, **Distribution** to **Gaussian**, and the click **OK**. Save the document with the name **sandDisplace.psd**. Create a new **1000x1000** px Photoshop document and then set the **Foreground** and **Background** colors as follows: **#c99754** and **#e6c09b**. Choose **Render | Clouds** from the **Filter** menu.

3. Choose **Filter Gallery | Texture | Texturizer** from the **Filter** menu and then use the **sandDisplace.psd** as **Texture**. Also, set **Scaling** to **100**, and **Relief** to **29**. Select **Light** to **Top Left** [Fig. T2] and then click **OK**. Fig. T3 shows the result.

4. Open the **crumpledPaper.jpg** and choose **Other | High Pass** from the **Filter** menu. Now, set **Radius** to **165** in the **High Pass** dialog box that appears and then click **OK** [Fig. T4]. Save the document as **crumpledPaper.psd**.

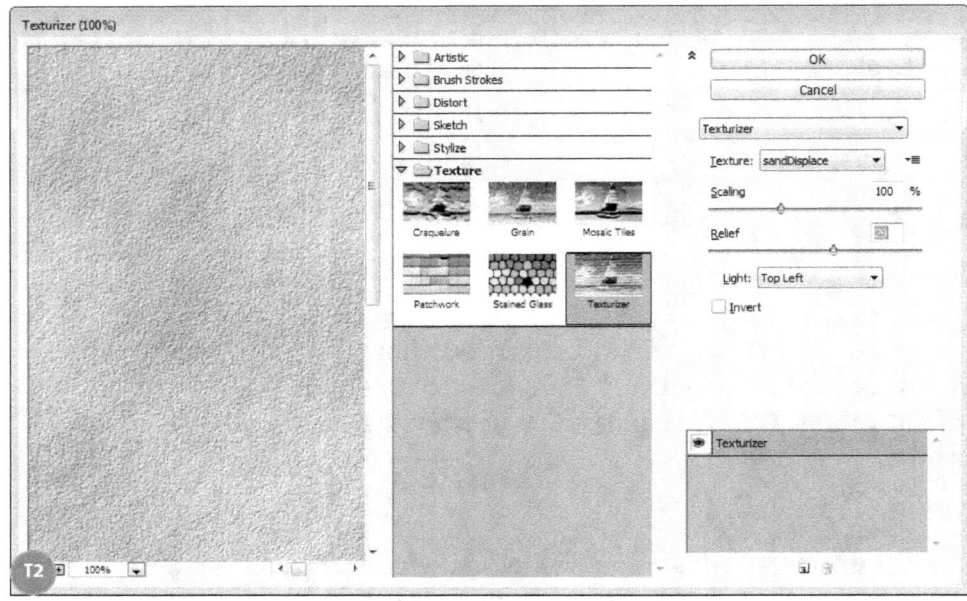

> **Note:** *crumpledPaper.jpg*
> **Image Courtesy:** *http://capturedbykc.deviantart.com/*
> **Download Link:** *http://www.deviantart.com/art/ 50-Paper-Textures-Bundle-358150111.*

5. Switch to the new document you created. Choose **Filter Gallery | Texture | Texturizer** from the **Filter** menu and then use the **crumpledPaper.psd** as **Texture**. Also, set **Scaling**

to **144**, and **Relief** to **46**. Select **Light** to **Top Left** [Fig. T5] and then click **OK**. Save the document.

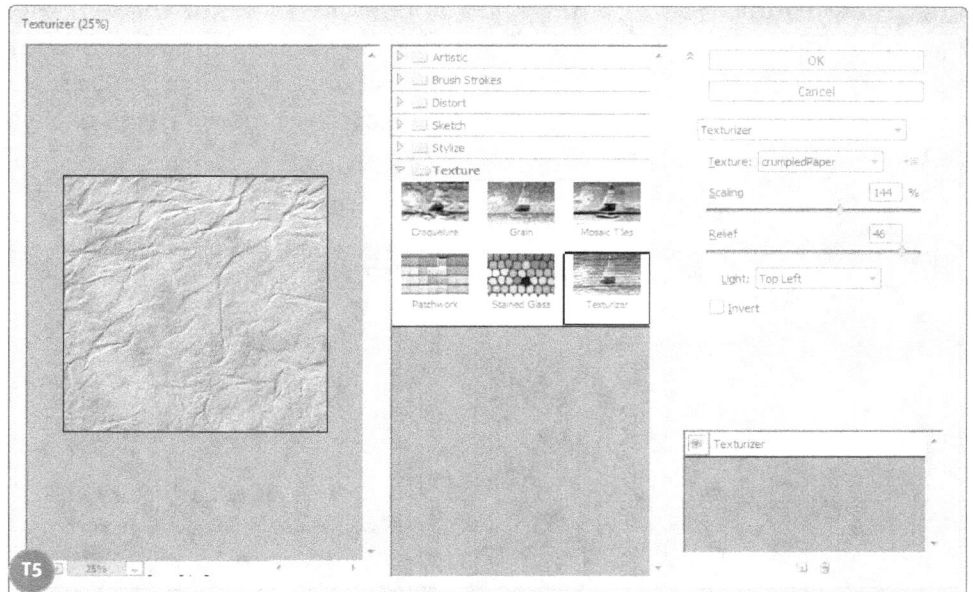

Tutorial 9: Creating an Organic Texture

In this tutorial, we will create an organic looking texture, Fig. T1.

The following table summarizes the tutorial:

Table T9	
Flow: *The following sequence will be used in this tutorial:* *1. Create a new Photoshop document. 2. Use the* **Difference Clouds, Emboss, Paint Daubs,** *and* **Plastic Wrap** *filters to create texture.*	
Keywords: Difference Clouds, Emboss, Paint Daubs, and Plastic Wrap	
Difficulty level	Beginner
Estimated time to complete	15 Minutes
Resources folder	**chapter-f5**
Final tutorial file	**f5_tut9_finish.psd**

Follow the steps given next:

1. Create a new **1000x1000** px Photoshop document then set the **Foreground** and **Background** colors to default values. Choose **Render | Difference Clouds** from the **Filter** menu. Apply this filter multiple time by pressing **Alt+Ctrl+F**, until you get a nice pattern [refer Fig. T2]. Unlock the **Background** layer. Create two more copies of **Layer 0** and name them as **Layer 1** and **Layer 2**, respectively.

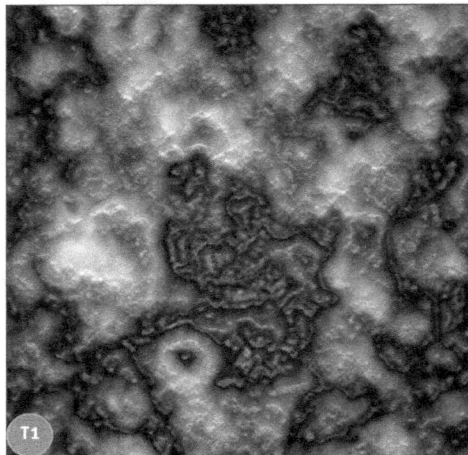
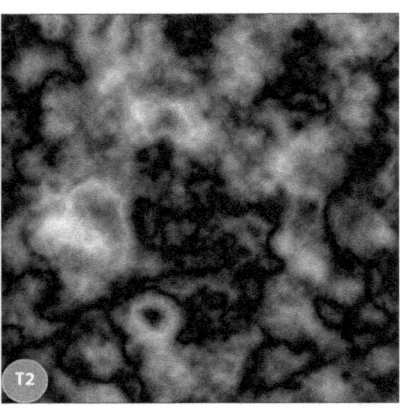

2. Turn off **Layer 1** and **Layer 2**. Ensure **Layer 0** is selected in the **Layers** panel and then choose **Filter Gallery | Artistic | Plastic Wrap** from the **Filter** menu and then set **Highlight Strength** to **11**, **Detail** to **9**, and **Smoothness** to **6** [refer Fig. T3]. Click **OK**.

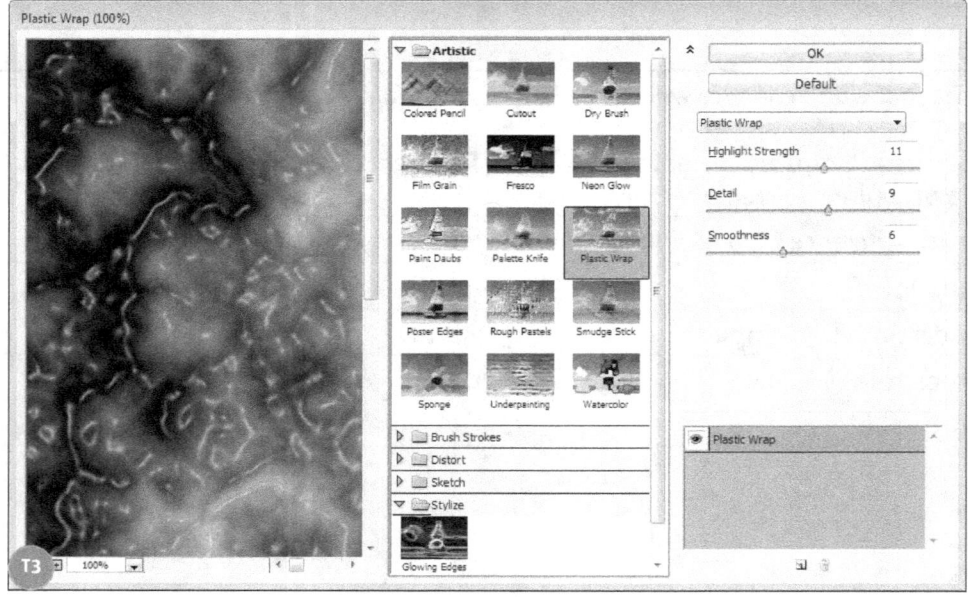

> **Note: Plastic Wrap Filter**
> This filter wraps the image in the shiny plastic, making the surface details more noticeable. The generated pattern may be different in your case as it depends on the base pattern that is created on applying filer multiple times.

3. Turn on **Layer 1** and select it in the **Layers** panel. Choose **Stylize | Emboss** from the **Filter** menu. In the **Emboss** dialog box that appears, set **Angle** to **90**, **Height** to **4**, and **Amount** to **500** [Fig. T4]. Click **OK**. Set **Blending Mode** to **Overlay** for **Layer 1**. Now, select **Layer 2** and make it visible. Choose **Filter Gallery | Artistic | Paint Daubs** from the **Filter** menu and then set **Brush Size** to **10**, **Sharpness** to **3**, and **Brush Type** to **Simple** [refer Fig. T5].

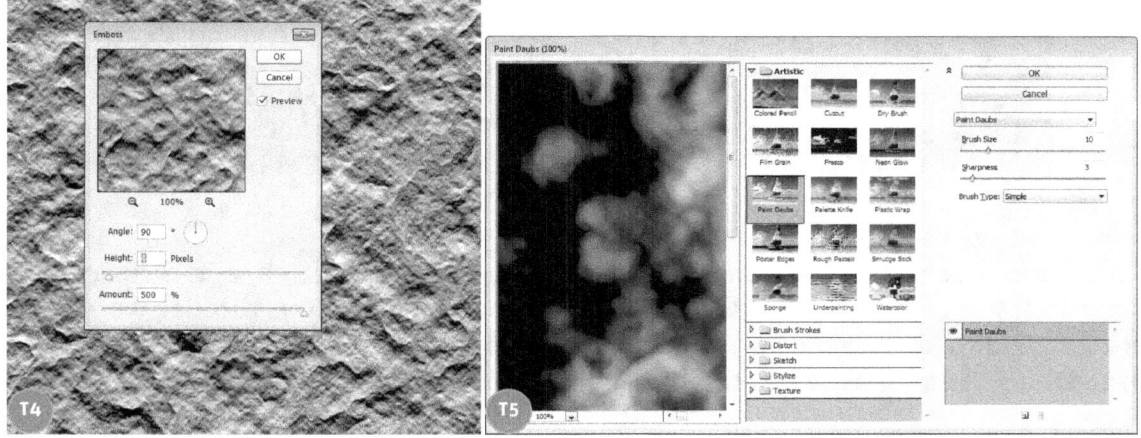

4. Click **OK**. Set **Blending Mode** to **Lighten** for **Layer 2**. Fig. T6 shows the result.

> **Note: Paint Daubs Filter**
> This filter produces a painterly effect using different brushes. The available brushes are **Simple, Light Rough, Dark Rough, Wide Sharp, Wide Blurry**, and **Sparkle** [refer to images given below].

5. Select **Layer 0** and then choose **Blur | Gaussian Blur** from the **Filter** menu. In the **Gaussian Blur** dialog box that opens, set **Radius** to **3** and then click **OK** [Fig. T7].

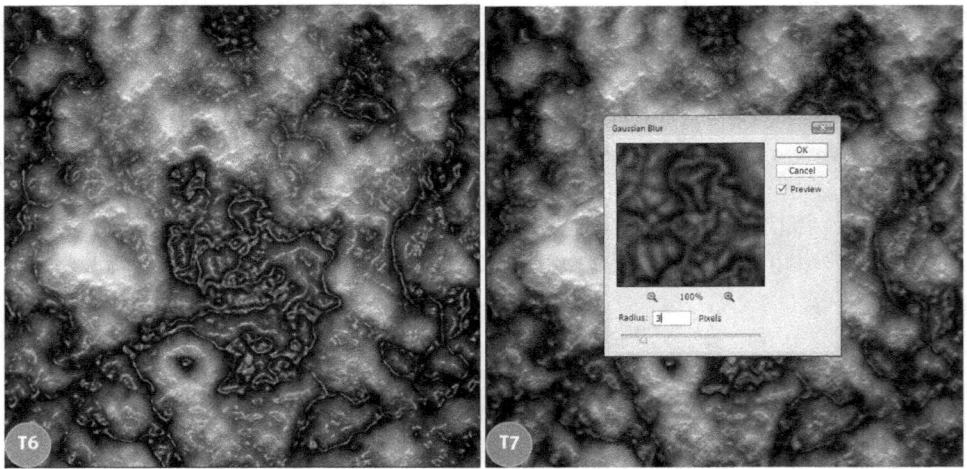

Tutorial 10: Creating custom diffuse, bump, reflection, and displacement maps

This tutorial deals with creating custom diffuse, bump, reflection, and displacement maps that you can use in any 3D application of your choice. In this tutorial, we will first create the diffuse map by converting an image to a seamless texture and then we will use various techniques to create other maps from the seamless diffuse map.

The following table summarizes the tutorial:

Table T10	
Flow: The following sequence will be used to create the custom diffuse, bump, reflection, and displacement maps: 1. Create a new Photoshop document. 2. Use the channel data to create custom maps.	
Keywords: Offset and Clone Stamp	
Difficulty level	Beginner
Estimated time to complete	15 Minutes
Resources folder	chapter-f5
Final tutorial file	f5_tut10_finish.psd

Follow the steps given next:

1. Open Photoshop. Create a **2000x2000** px document. Save the file as **concreteBare_Diffuse.psd**. Open **Concrete_L.jpg** and drag it to **concreteBare_Diffuse.psd** Photoshop file. Now, place **Concrete_L.jpg** as shown in Fig. T1. Rename the layer as **Base** [Fig. T2].

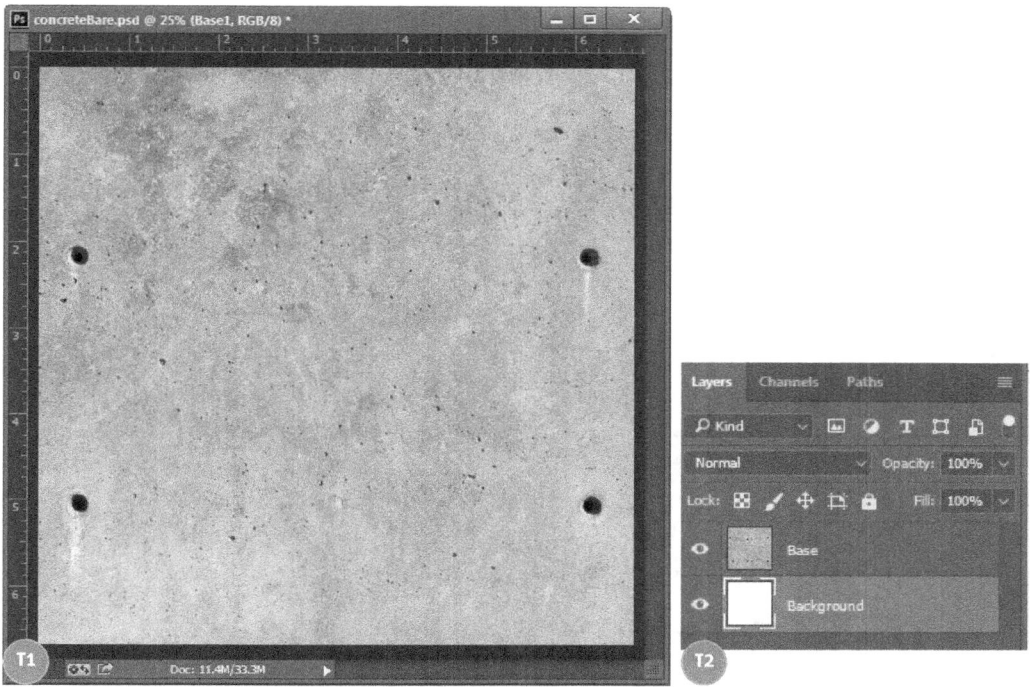

2. From the **Filter** menu, choose **Other | Offset** to open the **Offset** dialog box. In this dialog box, set **Horizontal** and **Vertical** to **1000**. Also, make sure **Wrap Around** is chosen in the **Undefined Areas** group.

You will see that the offset is not centered on the canvas even if I have set **Horizontal** and **Vertical** to **1000** units which is half the size of the document. It happens because **Offset** filter takes whole image into account not just the visible area of the canvas [Fig. T3]. Choose **Cancel** from the **Offset** dialog box. To overcome this issue, I will select the visible area of the image and then apply the **Offset** filter.

3. Press **Ctrl+A** to select the visible area of the image and then press **Ctrl+J** to create a layer from the selection. Rename the new layer as **Base1**. From the **Filter** menu, choose **Other | Offset** to open the **Offset** dialog box. In this dialog box, set **Horizontal** and **Vertical** to **1000** and then click **OK** to offset the texture [Fig. T4].

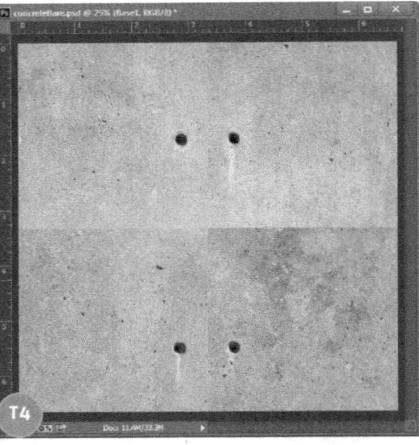

4. Create a copy of **Base** and then move it above **Base1** [Fig. T5]. Add a layer mask to the **Base copy** and fill it with **black** [Fig. T6]. Set **white** as active color and then make sure the layer mask is selected. Now, use a grunge or noise brush and paint on the seams using white color [Fig. T7].

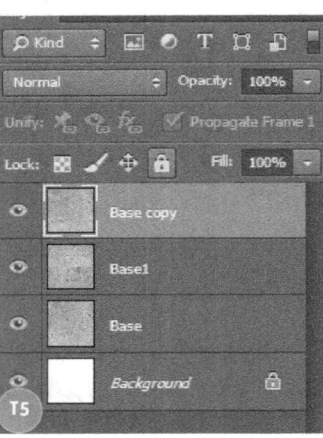
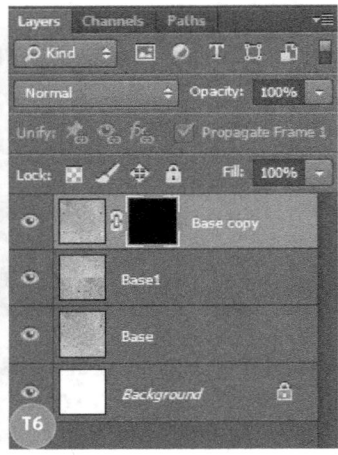

5. Now, choose a different noise brush and randomly paint to reveal some more texture. Choose **Flatten Image** from the **Layer** menu to collapse all layers. Create clones of holes on their opposite side using **Clone Stamp** tool [Fig. T8].

6. Now, add a **Levels** adjustment layer and adjust the levels [Fig. T9]. Make sure the layer mask of **Level 1** layer is selected. Now, paint black to get the some of the details back from the state prior to applying levels [Fig. T10].

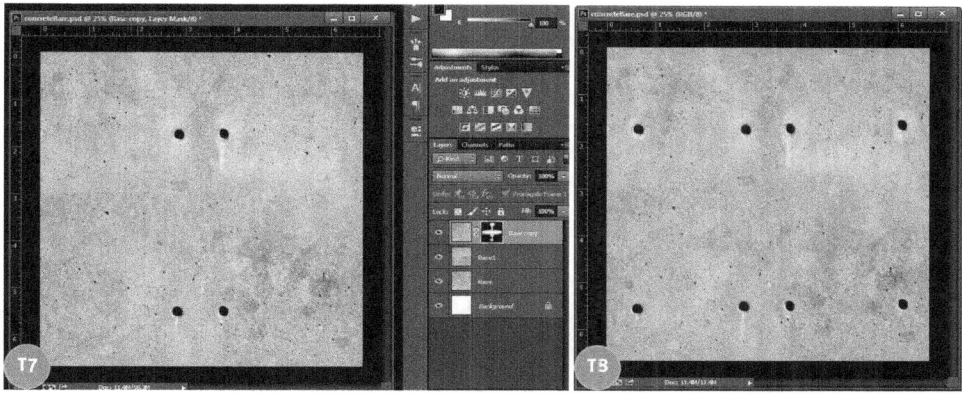

Note: Levels Command
The **Levels** command/adjustment layer allows you to make adjustment to the tonal range and color balance of an image. This command adjusts the intensity levels of shadows, midtones, and highlights of an image. The histogram that this command provides, gives you a visual feed for adjusting the key tones of the image [see the image on the right].

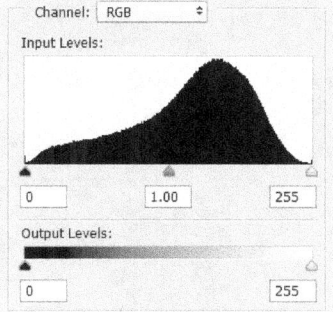

Tip: Correcting Exposure and Color Balance
You can quickly fix issues like color balance and incorrect exposure using the **Levels** command. The shortcut key to invoke this command is **Ctrl+L**.

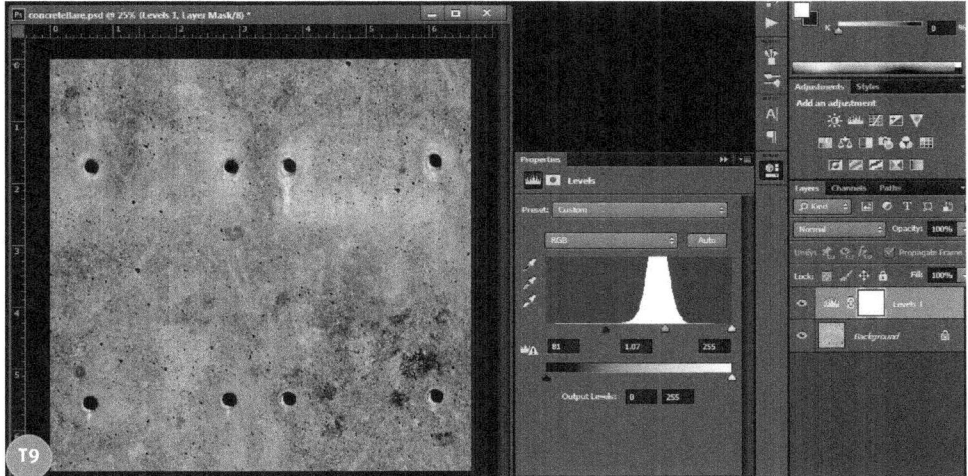

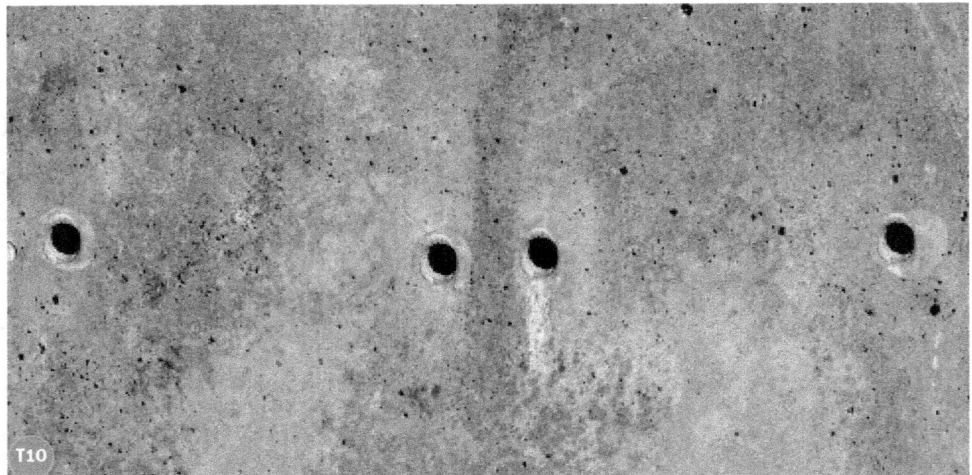

7. Open **Grunge_A.jpg** and place it on the **concreteBare_Diffuse.psd** image. Open the **Layer Style** dialog box and adjust the **Blend If** options as shown in Fig. T11 and then click **OK**. Add a layer mask to the grunge layer and make sure it is selected.

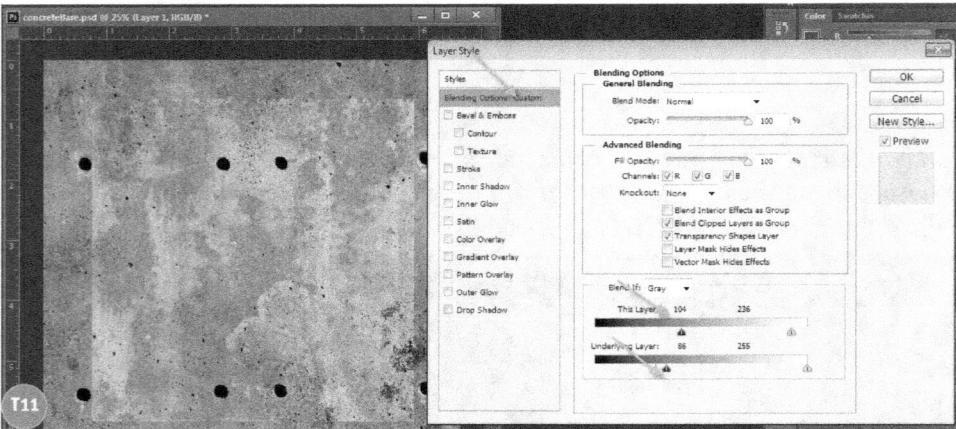

8. Now, paint with black color using a noise brush to get rid of the seams [Fig. T12]. Save the Photoshop file.

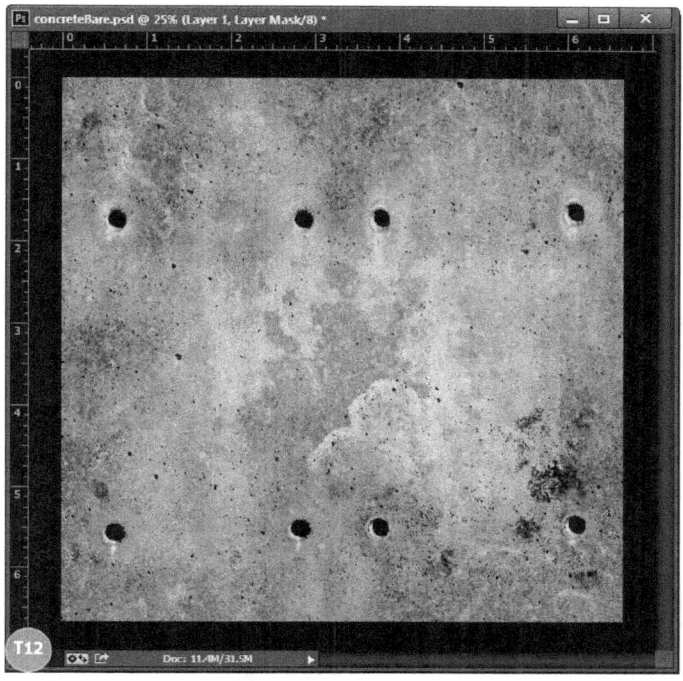

Tip: Adding Contrast to the Image
If any image does not use the full tonal range, you can use the **Shadow** and **Highlight** input sliders inward until they touch the end of histogram. See the before and after images given next.

Next, we will create the reflection map. You can create this map by desaturating the image [Shortcut: **Shift+Ctrl+U**] and then using levels to exaggerate contrast in the image. However, I like to use the blue channel of the image to create reflection map as this channel already has some contrast by default. Let's do it.

Note: The Desaturate Command
The **Desaturate** command is responsible for converting color values to the grayscale values. However, it does not change the color mode of the image. This command produces results similar to that of the **Hue/Saturation** command when you set **Saturation** to **-100**.

Warning: The Desaturate Command
*If you are working with a multi-layer document, the **Desaturate** command converts the selected layer to grayscale values.*

9. On the **Channels** panel, click the **Blue** layer. Press **Ctrl+A** and then **Shift+Ctrl+C** to copy the information. Now, create a new Photoshop document and press **Ctrl+V** to paste the data. **Shift+Ctrl+C** is the shortcut key for the **Copy Merged** command.

This command copies merged data of all visible layers in the selected area. In contrast, the **Copy** command copies the selected area on the active layer. Add a **Levels** adjustment layer and exaggerate contrast in the image [Fig. T13]. Save the file as **concreteBare_Reflection.psd**.

10. Similarly, to create the bump map, use the red channel information and adjust levels to lighten the tone [Fig. T14]. If you want more details, you can use the **Brightness and Contrast** adjustment to boost the contrast [Fig. T15]. Save the file as **concreteBare_Bump.psd**.

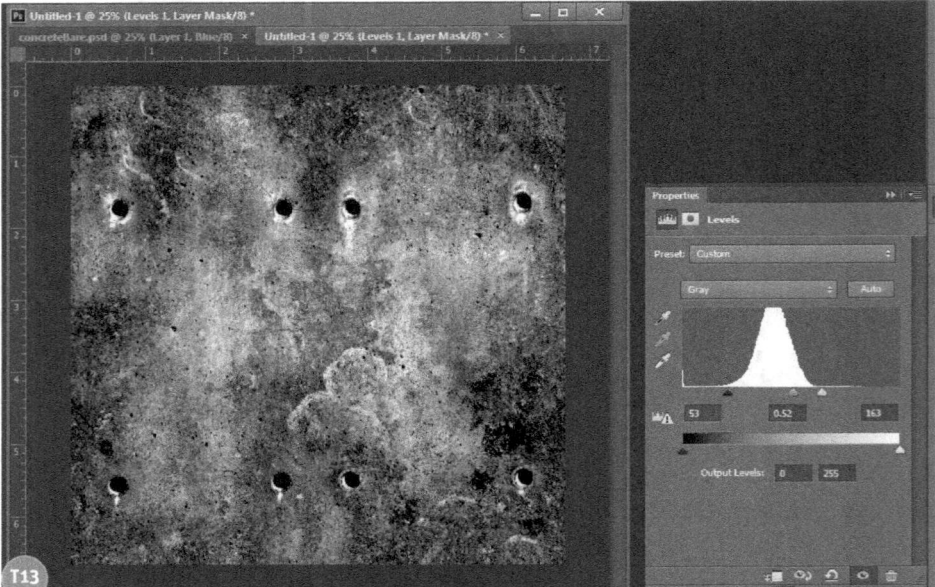

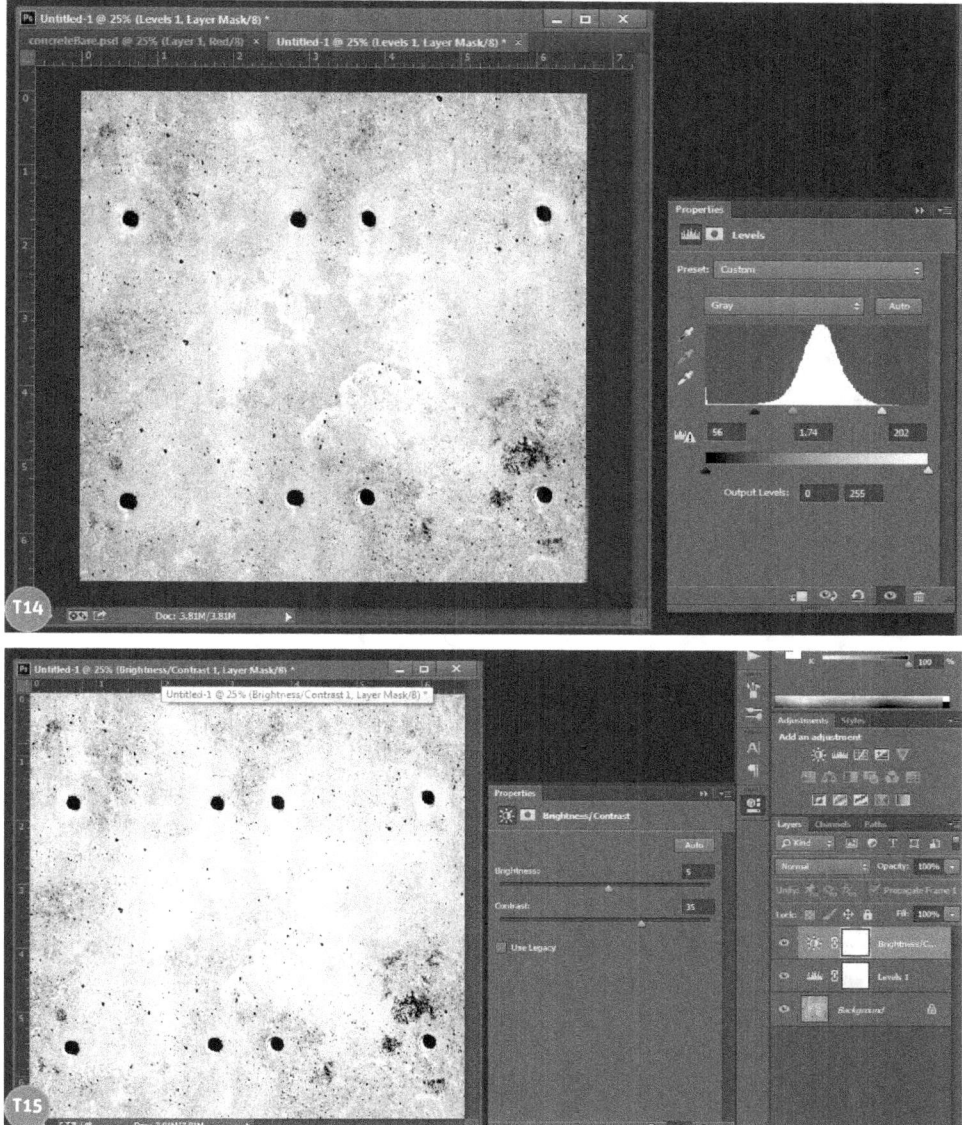

To create the displacement map, copy the bump map and paste it in a new document. Add a **Levels** adjustment layer and adjust levels until you get the cleaner holes [Fig. T16]. Keep in mind that the white area will be displaced on rendering, the black area will be left alone.

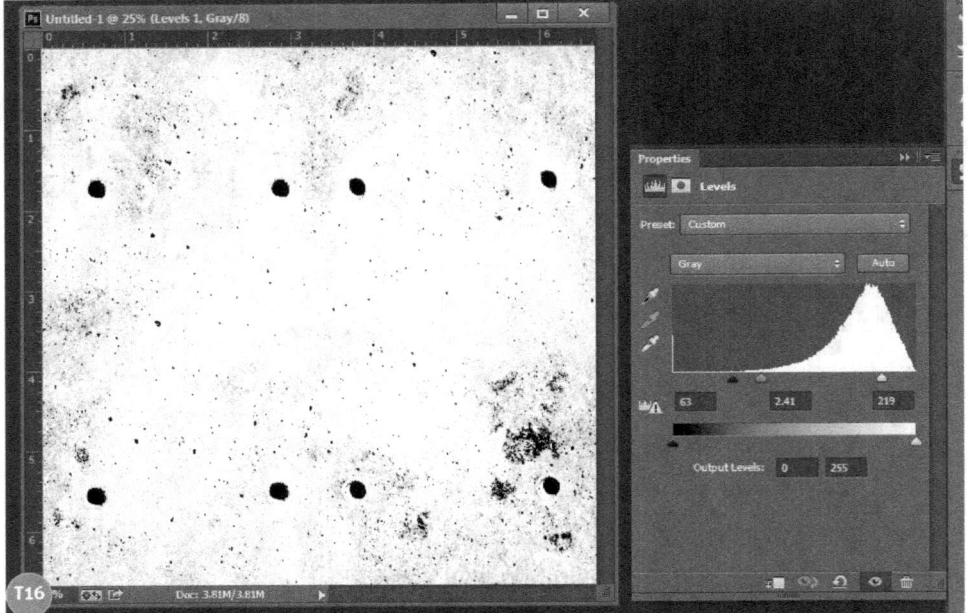

11. Blur the image with the **Gaussian Blur** filter with the strength of **1.3** for smooth displacement map. Save the file as **concreteBare_Displacement.psd**.

Summary
In this chapter:

- 10 tutorials covering texture creation techniques.
- Covers the following filters: **Difference Clouds, High Pass, Add Noise, Gaussian Blur, Wind, Texturizer, Halftone Pattern, Sumi-e, Water Paper, Stained Glass, Motion Blur, Emboss, Paint Daubs, Offset**, and **Plastic Wrap**

Index

A

Adjustment Layers
 Brightness/Contrast F2-10
 Curves F4-15
 Hue and Saturation F3-5, F4-15
 Level F3-9, F4-15, F5-30, F5-34, F5-35

C

Commands
 Calculations F4-10, F4-11
 Color Balance F2-10
 Copy Merged F3-9
 Desaturate F5-33, F5-34
 Equalize F5-5
 Exposure F5-4, F5-5, F5-31
 Fade F4-8
 Flatten Image F3-10
 Flip Horizontal F4-14
 Hue/Saturation F5-5, F5-33
 Levels F5-31
 Rasterize Layer Style F4-4
 Shadows/Highlights F2-9
Convert to Smart Object F3-3

F

Filter Gallery F1-3
 Offset filter F3-8
Filters
 16-Bit Images Compatible F1-2
 32-bit Images Compatible F1-2
 Add Noise , F4-6, F5-6, F5-19
 Average F5-3
 Chrome F4-1, F4-14, F4-15, F4-16, F4-17, F4-18, F4-24
 Clouds F4-2, F5-3, F4-16, F5-23, F5-25, F5-26
 Difference Clouds F5-2
 Emboss F4-7, F4-8, F4-12, F4-8, F5-17, F5-21
 Fibers F4-22
 Gaussian Blur F3-3, F4-21, F5-3, F5-6, F5-7, F5-12, F5-13, F5-28, F5-36
 Halftone Pattern F4-1, F4-6, F5-10, F5-11, F5-12, F4-24
 High Pass F3-2
 Lens Flare F4-1, F4-10, F4-12, F4-13, F4-24
 Maximum F3-5
 Minimum F3-5
 Motion Blur F4-1, F4-2, F4-3, F4-4, F4-7, F4-8, F4-19, F4-20, F4-2, F5-18, F4-24
 Paint Daubs F5-27
 Patchwork F4-2
 Plaster F4-1, F4-16, F4-22, F4-24
 Plastic Wrap F5-25, F5-26, F5-27
 Polar Coordinates F4-14
 Radial Blur F4-22
 Shake Reduction F2-2
  Artifact Suppression option F2-5
  Blur Direction Tool F2-4
  Blur Estimation Tool F2-3
  Detail loupe F2-4, F2-5
  Smoothing option F2-5
 Smart Sharpen F2-11
 Sprayed Strokes F4-22
 Stained Glass F5-14, F5-17, F5-20
 Sumi-e Filter F5-14
 Texturizer F5-10, F5-11, F5-14, F5-15, F5-18, F5-19, F5-20, F5-21, F5-22, F5-23, F5-24
 Trace Contour F4-1, F4-3, F4-4, F4-6, F4-7, F4-8, F4-24
 Twirl F4-1, F4-4, F4-5, F4-8, F4-19, F4-20, F4-23, F4-24
 Unsharp Mask F2-5, F2-6, F2-8, F2-11
 Water Paper F4-6, F5-11
 Wave F4-1, F4-12, F4-13, F4-14, F4-16, F4-17, F4-18, F4-19, F4-20, F4-21, F4-24

Wind filter F5-7

T

Tools
    Clone Stamp Tool F3-8, F3-10, F3-12
    Crop Tool F3-7
    Healing Brush Tool F3-10
    Magic Wand Tool , F4-8, F5-17

www.ingramcontent.com/pod-product-compliance
Lightning Source LLC
Chambersburg PA
CBHW062220220526
45471CB00009B/3283